AMERICAN STEAM
LOCOMOTIVES

BY PAUL NORTH

GALLERY BOOKS
An Imprint of W. H. Smith Publishers Inc.
112 Madison Avenue
New York City 10016

Contents

WRITTEN BY PAUL NORTH
EDITED BY THOMAS E. BONSALL
GRAPHIC DESIGN BY JUDY CRAVEN-MADISON
FILM PRODUCTION BY HAHN GRAPHICS

© Copyright 1988 in U.S.A. by Bookman Dan!, Inc.
Published in the United States of America by
Bookman Publishing, an Imprint of Bookman Dan Inc.,
P. O. Box 13492, Baltimore, MD 21203

Exclusive Distribution by Gallery Books,
an Imprint of W. H. Smith Publishers Inc.,
112 Madison Avenue, New York City, NY 10016

ISBN 0-8317-5599-7

Printed in the United States of America

Preface

There have been many books written about steam locomotives. Most seem to be written for hardcore steam enthusiasts and, while there is nothing wrong with that, it seemed to Bookman Publishing that a book oriented more toward the layman might be in order--a book perhaps more inclined to discuss the historical development and significance of steam locomotives than the minute technical details of their design, manufacture and operation. This is not to say that there has been a casual attitude taken toward the completeness and accuracy of the material contained herein. Quite the opposite. Moreover, for the sake of authenticity, an attempt has been made to use original art and photography as much as possible. There are, as a result, illustrations here that have never before been published in book form and will, in many cases, be of keen interest even to the dyed-in-the-wool buffs. In any event, we believe that his book approaches an oft-told tale with a refreshing point of view. We hope you will agree.

The night scene, left, shows the Boston & Maine Railroad's locomotive number 1455 letting off steam. The 2-6-0 Mogul type was built in Manchester, New Hampshire, in 1907.

The photo on the previous pages is rather poignant for a couple of reasons. First, it is a sort of changing-of-the-guard type of picture--out with the old and in with the new, as it were, except that there are many who think progress missed a step when it consigned the steam locomotive to the scrap heap. The second reason this photograph is significant is that the locomotives themselves are of more than passing interest. The steam locomotive is Wilmington & Western's number 98, while the other is Amtrak's AEM-7 number 900. The two were participants in the rededication of Wilmington, Delaware's, passenger station on June 8, 1984. A few months later, Amtrak 900 was involved in the worst wreck in Amtrak history at Chase, Maryland, between Baltimore and Wilmington, with a loss of 17 lives.

CHECKS that have come every year for 100 years

SINCE its founding 100 years ago, the Pennsylvania Railroad has paid to its employees, stockholders and bondholders approximately twelve and a half billion dollars.

Never once over that century has it failed to meet a financial obligation when due.

To its employees the Pennsylvania has paid in wages a sum exceeding ten billion dollars.

To stockholders, it has paid a cash return in every year since 1847—a total of a billion and a quarter dollars.

To bondholders—individuals, and insurance companies, savings banks, trust companies, representing the savings of many millions of individuals—it has paid in interest more than a billion dollars.

From the beginning, the Pennsylvania has been a railroad built by the people for the people. The money to construct it as the shortest route between East and West came from people of all walks of life in the form of subscriptions to shares of $50 each, payable in ten $5 installments. Today, with 13,167,754 shares outstanding, the average holding is only $61\frac{1}{4}$ shares, and of the 214,995 stockholders of the railroad 106,139—or more than 49%—are women.

Thus, not only has the Pennsylvania Railroad served the American people through continually improving transportation at low cost—but through wages, dividends and interest (plus huge purchases of materials in the area served)—it has contributed vitally to the prosperity of communities and to the welfare and economic security of many thousands of American citizens.

PENNSYLVANIA RAILROAD

1846   1946

ONE HUNDRED YEARS OF   TRANSPORTATION PROGR

CHAPTER ONE

A Brief History of the
Steam Locomotive in America

America's romance with the rails began even before the turn of the 19th century. The earliest railroads, primitive affairs as they were, were horse-drawn. In fact, horse power was the prevalent method of locomotion well into what we normally think of as the steam era.

The first railroad in the United States is said to have been a short inclined track used as early as 1795 to convey brick and other clay products from kilns on Beacon Hill, Boston, to a street below. Later, in 1807, Silas Whitney built a short railway at the same location. The rails were of wood.

In 1809, Thomas Leiper built a tramway to connect his quarry at Crum Creek, Delaware County, Pennsylvania, with tidewater on Ridley Creek. This roadway later became a part of the

pioneering Baltimore & Ohio Railroad. About 1811, a tramroad was constructed on Falling's Creek, in Chesterfield County, Virginia, to furnish transportation for a powder mill. In 1818, another tramroad was built at Bear Creek Furnace, Armstrong County, Pennsylvania. Still later, in 1825, a tramroad was built at Nashua, New Hampshire. None of these early lines, of course,

The advertisement, opposite, was run on the occasion of the Pennsylvania Railroad's hundredth anniversary in 1946. The other half of the ad appears on the cover of this book.

The Fryeburg Horse Rail Road was still in operation at the turn of the Century when the photograph, above, was taken.

The Stourbridge Lion, above, now resides in the Smithsonian. Managed by Horatio Allen, it was the first steam · locomotive ever run commercially in America. That momentous event took place on August 8, 1829.

Below, the Tom Thumb of the Baltimore & Ohio Railroad. In August, 1830, near Baltimore, Maryland, it lost a celebrated race with a horse-drawn train.

were steam powered, but the basic idea--a road of rails--was there.

The first steam railroad to be conceived in the United States came in 1815. John Stevens, of Hoboken, New Jersey, obtained a state charter to build and operate a steam railroad between New Brunswick and Trenton, New Jersey. Although the charter expired without the railroad being built, the idea persisted and, on March 7, 1823, the New Jersey Railroad & Transportation Company (later to become a part of the Pennsylvania Railroad) was chartered to build across the state. It was not until January 1, 1839, however, that the railroad was finally opened, between New Brunswick and Trenton.

Incorporated by the Massachusetts legislature March 4, 1826, the Granite Railway Company, was the first railway corporation actually to build and operate a railroad in this country. The Granite Railway, originally of 5-foot gauge and about 3 miles in length, was built by Gridley Bryant to convey huge blocks and columns of granite from a quarry in Quincy to Milton, on the Neponset

River, for use in the construction of the famous Bunker Hill Monument. The road was opened October 7, 1826, with horses supplying the power.

The Mauch Chunk Railroad, extending a distance of nine miles from the coal mines in northeastern Pennsylvania to the Lehigh River, was completed in 1827. At the time, it was the longest and most important railroad operating in America. It was a combination of level and inclined planes. A "switchback" track was added in 1844 to facilitate transportation and to eliminate the use of mules for the "up" movement of the cars. Gravity was used for the downward trip. The railroad ceased operating as a means of coal transportation about 1870 but continued operating as a famous scenic passenger railway until it was finally abandoned in 1931.

Although these early railroads can justly claim credit for pioneering rail transportation in the United States, their motive power was still supplied by horses, men or, in a few cases, simple gravity. Railroads in the modern sense had to await the development of practical steam locomotives.

The first steam engine to run on rails in America was built by John Stevens in 1825 and was operated on a circular experimental track on his

The Baltimore & Ohio Railroad was organized in 1827, thus becoming America's first passenger railroad. When, in August, 1835, the B&O formally opened its branch between Baltimore and Washington, DC, four steam locomotives were placed in service: the George Washington, the John Adams, the Thomas Jefferson and the James Madison. The Thomas Jefferson is shown above. The 40-mile run between Baltimore and Washington took about two-and-a-half hours.

estate at Hoboken, New Jersey. Despite the exciting potential of this "first," Stevens' engine was never put to practical use. Indeed, it was not American steam engines, but ones built in Great Britain that achieved the next step in railroad development.

Of the first of four English-built locomotives brought to America, the "Stourbridge Lion" is the only one about which much is known. The "Lion" arrived in New York by sailing vessel on May 13, 1829. Driven by Horatio Allen, the young civil engineer of the Delaware & Hudson Canal Company, the engine made a trial run at Honesdale, Pennsylvania, on August 8, 1829, but it was found to be too heavy for the track and was converted to stationary use.

HAVE ARRIVED

AT _____

Speaking of Railroads...

As important a part of American life as the railroad were at the height of the steam era, it is not surprising that they became a focus of all sorts of popular expression, from humor to songs. The postcard, above, was sold at train stations for arriving travelers to mail to friends and loved ones. The novelty card, right, provides an example of German ethnic humor, a type that used to be quite prevalent but is now virtually unknown.

The list of popular songs that used railroad themes would probably require a book this size to list. From the "Ballad of Casey Jones" to the "Chattanooga Choo-Choo," they ran the gamut of human emotions and experiences. The song that made the top of the charts in 1904 (about the time of these cards) was "Meet Me In St. Louis, Louis" about a man who comes home from work only to find his wife has packed up and abandoned him to take a train trip to the 1904 Louisiana Purchase Exposition in St. Louis. And, so it goes...

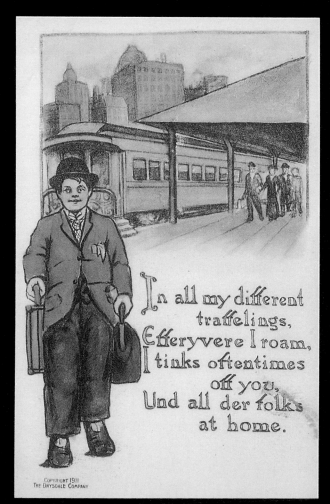

In all my different traffelings, Efferyvere I roam, I tinks oftentimes off you, Und all der folks at home.

COPYRIGHT 1911
THE DRYSDALE COMPANY

The first American-built locomotive actually to be operated on a common-carrier railroad in the United States was the celebrated "Tom Thumb," an experimental engine built in 1829 by Peter Cooper, a New York ironmaster, and given a trial run on the Baltimore & Ohio Railroad, at Baltimore, in September of that year. The Tom Thumb was the centerpiece of a famous race, on August 25, 1830, with a horse-drawn car. The purpose was to test the comparative speeds of the two modes of locomotion and was run a distance of 13 miles between Baltimore and Ellicott's Mills, now Ellicott City, Maryland. The horse-drawn train won, incidentally. It was one of the last hurrahs of the horse in rail transportation, though, but added a colorful chapter to American railway history.

Following the retirement of the Tom Thumb, the "York," built by Phineas Davis, in York, Pennsylvania, was tried out on the Baltimore & Ohio Railroad on July 12, 1831. It was placed in service at Baltimore shortly thereafter.

The Baltimore & Ohio was the first railroad to serve as a public conveyor of passengers and freight. On July 4, 1828--not coincidentally America's Independence Day--Charles Carroll, then 91 years of age and the only living signer of the Declaration of Independence, had participated in the historic ceremony of the laying of the first stone in the construction of the Baltimore & Ohio at Baltimore, Maryland. The Founding Father delivered a speech on that occasion in which he said, in part:

"I consider this among the most important acts of my life; second only to my signing the Declaration of Independence, if even it be second to that."

The first revenue passengers on the Baltimore & Ohio were not actually carried until January 7, 1830. The road was opened for regular freight and passenger traffic between Baltimore and Ellicott's Mills on May 24, 1830. Despite the experiments with the Tom Thumb, horses were originally used for motive power.

The first steam locomotive to be placed

The John Bull, below, was the first steam locomotive to run on rails in America. Built by John Stevens, it was run on an experimental track at Stevens' estate in New Jersey in 1825. The John Bull was never put to practical, commercial use, however, and the first practical American locomotives were of British manufacture.

in regular service on any American railroad, and the first to haul a train of cars, was the "Best Friend of Charleston," built at the West Point Foundry in New York. Having completed six miles of its line from Charleston, formal opening of the railroad inaugurating regular service, took place on December 25, 1830, after trains of four or five passenger cars had made trial trips on December 14-

The Best Friend of Charleston, above, was the first steam locomotive placed in regular service in America. This is a reconstruction.

A comparison between early American and British locomotives can be seen from the artist's drawing, below, of the Liverpool & Manchester Railroad in 1830.

Opposite, an early C&O advertisement.

British locomotive *Planet* hauls passenger train across stone bridge on Liverpool and Manchester Railroad — 1830

Above, Ross Winans' Camel, built in 1869 for the B&O. Winans was the inventor of the camel-back type of locomotive which was to become quite popular as a freight hauler.

Below, the original John Bull now resides in the Smithsonian Institution in Washington, DC.

15, 1830. The second steam locomotive to be placed in regular service, the "West Point," also built at West Point Foundry, was likewise placed in service on the South Carolina Railroad, on July 15, 1831.

In the early stages of their development, both the Baltimore & Ohio and the South Carolina railroads tried cars equipped with sails, and also with treadmills driven by horses. It is reported that one strange contrivance tried out by the Baltimore & Ohio was condemned after it had been derailed by a trespassing cow.

The "DeWitt Clinton," the first locomotive to be placed in regular service in New York State, and also built at West Point Foundry, made its initial run on the Mohawk & Hudson Railroad (later to become a part of the New York Central). This historic event took place from Albany to Schenectady on August 9, 1831.

The "John Bull," built in England, was delivered to the Camden & Amboy Railroad on August 31, 1831, and was placed in regular service at Bordentown, New Jersey, November 12th of that year. The John Bull was the first locomotive to run

on what was to become the Pennsylvania Railroad lines. The same year also saw the Camden & Amboy record another first: the first use of the modern railroad spike. Spikes of various designs had been used from the earliest days of railway development, but the hooked-head spike was to become the standard type used by railroads throughout the world to fasten steel rails to crossties. This type was designed in 1831 by Robert L. Stevens, the first president of the Camden & Amboy Railroad.

The Pontchartrain Railroad, a 5-mile line extending from Elysian Fields Street, New Orleans, to the shore of Lake Pontchartrain at Milneburg, was the first railroad in the Mississippi Valley. It was chartered January 20, 1830, and was opened for horse-powered operation April 23, 1831. The Pontchartrain Railroad's first steam locomotive, the Pontchartrain," was built in England and placed in regular service September, 1832. For many years, until its abandonment in 1935, the road was a part of the Louisville & Nashville Railroad.

The first locomotive equipped with a cab--and a very crude one at that--was the "Samuel

Above, the Satilla, a locomotive built by the Rogers locomotive works for the Atlantic and Gulf Railroad in 1860. This locomotive has been restored and is in the possession of the Henry Ford Museum (Edison Institute) at Greenfield Village.
Below, a very early 2-2-2.

D. Ingham" built by Eastwick & Harrison of Philadelphia for the Beaver Meadow Railroad (later the Lehigh Valley) in Pennsylvania in 1835-36. It was at about this time that rail service first came to Washington, DC.

The formal opening of the Washington Branch of the Baltimore & Ohio Railroad, between Baltimore and the Nation's Capital, was celebrated on August 25, 1835. Four gayly bedecked passenger trains from Baltimore--drawn by locomotives appropriately named "George Washington," "John Adams," "Thomas Jefferson" and "James Madison," and bearing a distinguished company--entered Washington on that date. In the early days, trains made the 40-mile run between Baltimore and Washington in about 2-1/2 hours. (The fastest Amtrak Metroliner makes the trip in about 40 minutes today, which doesn't seem like much of an improvement in a century-and-a-half.) By 1838, it was possible to journey from Washington to New York by rail, but with a few changes of cars en route. Indeed, for many years there was no direct rail connection at Baltimore and it was necessary to transfer railcars by horse from one line to the other.

William F. Harnden conceived the idea of opening a regular express service for banking houses, merchants and other business interests in New York and Boston. Harnden was an early passenger train conductor who came up with the idea after a few years in the service of the Boston & Worcester Railroad (later a part of the New York Central). An advertisement of February 23, 1839, in the Boston newspapers announced his "Boston and New York Express Package Car." Harnden also entered into a contract with the Boston & Providence Railroad (later part of the New York, New Haven & Hartford) and a steamship company plying between New York and Providence, to carry his business over their lines.

Starting on March 4, 1839, with a large carpetbag, Harnden, the first to carry express between cities as far apart as New York and Boston, traveled regularly between these two points. His business grew rapidly. Later a special package car was placed in service, offices were

COMPLETION OF THE PACIFIC RAILROAD—MEETING OF LOCOMOTIVE
[PHOTOGRAPHED BY SA

opened in New York and Boston, assistants were employed and the service was extended to Philadelphia and other cities. Among other early express ventures were those of Henry F. Wells and William Fargo operating to the West, Alvin F. Adams operating to the South, and Earle & Prew in New England.

The first rail connection between an Atlantic port and the Great Lakes was accomplished in 1842 when a chain of short railroads (all of which became

NION AND CENTRAL PACIFIC LINES: THE ENGINEERS SHAKE HANDS.
GER, SALT LAKE CITY.]

Above, the spanning of the continent was achieved in 1869 at Promontory Point, Utah, barely 40 years after the Tom Thumb. It was a truly epochal event and was undoubtedly the biggest news story since the end of the Civil War four years before. All across the nation--reported a contemporary observer--"Whistles were blown, bells were rung, guns were fired, processions were formed, and speeches became the order of the day. Congratulations were showered upon officials of the successful companies. Editors joined in a paean of praise. In truth, the completion of the first transcontinental road marked an epoch!"

Waters" was between Charleston and Chattanooga, on the Tennessee River. The final link in this route (later to become a part of the Nashville, Chattanooga & St. Louis) was opened on May 9, 1850. The Ohio River was reached from the East at Pittsburgh, by the Pennsylvania Railroad, on December 10, 1852, and at Wheeling, West Virginia, by the Baltimore & Ohio Railroad on December 24, 1852.

The first rail route between the Eastern seaboard and the Mississippi River was completed when the Chicago, Rock Island & Pacific reached Rock Island, Illinois, on February 22, 1853. The first such route through the South was completed when the Memphis & Charleston (later the Southern Railway) was opened to Memphis, Tennessee, on April 1, 1857. A "middle route," connecting East St. Louis with Cincinnati and Baltimore, was completed with the opening of the Ohio & Mississippi (later to become a part of the Baltimore & Ohio) on June 4, 1857.

The first locomotive to reach Chicago (destined to become the world's greatest railroad center) was the "Pioneer," built in 1836. It arrived by sailing vessel on October 10, 1848, for service on the Galena & Chicago Union Railroad (later the Chicago & North Western). The "Pioneer" made its initial run out of Chicago on October 25th of that year. The first train from the East entered Chicago over the Northern Indiana Railroad (later the New York Central) in the Spring of 1852.

The costs of using these early railroads

parts of the New York Central) was completed between Boston and Buffalo, via Albany. The first through line railroad from the East to the Great Lakes was that of the New York & Erie (later the Erie) which opened from Piermont, on the Hudson River, to Dunkirk, on Lake Erie, on May 14-15, 1851. The line--of six-foot gauge--was then both the broadest railroad in the United States and the longest line in the world.

The second rail connection to the "Western

19

The Locomotive, left is Boston & Maine Railroad's number 494 as seen on display at the 1939 New York World's Fair. An American 4-4-0 type built by Manchester Locomotive Works in Manchester, New Hampshire, in 1892, it was presented by the B&M to a group of steam buffs who were interested in preserving it.

Two Short-Line Railroads for Today's Steam Enthusiasts

In recent years, the continuing enthusiasm for trains of the steam era has led to the preservation of many locomotives and the preservation and creation of dozens of short-line steam railroads. On these roads, the old steam locomotives can be seen in operation and experienced once again.

The Historic Wilmington & Western Steam Railroad is an example of a road that fell into disuse only to be rescued from oblivion by a dedicated band of steam enthusiasts. Chartered in 1867 and opened in 1872, the Wilmington & Western carried passengers and freight for nearly 100 years along its short, but particularly scenic, route before surburban residential development caught up with it. Its usefulness as a freight line ending and its survival threatened, it was transformed some 20 years ago into a short-line railroad for steam enthusiasts. Listed in the National Register of Historic Places, the Wilmington & Western operates a regular schedule of departures from March through December. Information can be obtained by writing the Wilmington & Western Railroad, P. O. Box 5787, Wilmington, Delaware 19808. Three of the Wilmington & Western's past and present locomotives are illustrated in this book:

Number 92, on pages 20-21, a 2-6-0 Mogul type was built in 1910 by the Canadian Locomotive Company for the Canadian National Railways. Number 98, on pages 24-25, is a 4-4-0 American type built in 1909. Number 37, on pages 44-45, is a 2-8-2 Mikado type built in 1924 by the American Locomotive Company (Edward Feathers photo).

The oldest of the popular short-lines is the Strasburg Rail Road in Strasburg, Pennsylvania. It runs steam trains daily May through October and on a reduced schedule during most of the other months of the year. An added inducement to visit Strasburg is the Railroad Museum of Pennsylvania, which happens to be located just across the road. Information can be obtained by writing the Strasburg Rail Road, P. O. Box 96, Strasburg, Pennsylvania 17575. Two of the Strasburg Rail Road's current attractions are shown in this book:

Pennsylvania locomotive number 7002, on pages 108-109, is truly an historic train among historic trains. An E-7 Class Atlantic built in 1902, it was from the same class as the famous 7002 that set a world speed record in 1905 of 127.1 miles per hour. That particular locomotive was later scrapped, but the number was assigned to the present engine for display at the 1939 New York World's Fair. This locomotive belongs to the Railroad Museum of Pennsylvania and is run by Strasburg Rail Road.

Strasburg locomotive number 90, on pages 110-111, is a 2-10-0 Decapod built by Baldwin Locomotive Works in 1924 for the Great Western. (Both Strasburg Rail Road photos are by James R. Moody.)

were not cheap--even in absolute dollars. Doggett's "Railroad Guide and Gazette of 1848" gives the average revenue per ton-mile as 8.97 cents for first class freight and 6.16 cents for second-class freight, contrasted with an average of approximately 1.25 cents per ton-mile in 1948. Revenue per passenger-mile was reported by Doggett as 3.51 cents, contrasted with about 2.30 cents in 1948. These figures, of course, do not even begin to take into account the difference in purchasing power between the dollar in 1848 and the dollar in 1948.

The story of the development of the telegraph--a book in itself--was inextricably entwined with the development of the railroad. One of the earliest telegraph lines built for commercial use closely followed the Erie Railroad tracks across New York State. On September 22, 1851, Charles Minot, Superintendent of the Erie, was on a west-bound train which drew into a siding at Turner (now Harriman), New York, to allow an east-bound train to pass. The train, however, was late. Minot went to the telegraph office and wired ahead to locate the missing train. Learning that the train had not arrived at Goshen, 13 miles west, Minot sent a telegram ordering that the train be held there. He then instructed the waiting train to proceed to Goshen where it would meet the east-bound train. The locomotive engineer is said to have refused to take such a risk, whereupon Minot climbed into the cab and personally drove the engine to Goshen where the east-bound train was waiting. This is the first instance on record of the telegraph being used for train dispatching.

Still later, the railroads were to participate

in the development of the telephone. The world's first telephone message was transmitted by the inventor, Dr. Alexander Graham Bell, on March 10, 1876. Little more than a year later, at Altoona, Pennsylvania, on May 21, 1877, Bell's assistants began tests which resulted in the permanent installation of telephones in the Pennsylvania Railroad shops at that point--the first trial and use of the telephone for railroad purposes.

Below, Sante Fe engine number 2230. This 0-6-0 locomotive (photographed in 1901) was typical of the type run by the Sante Fe system in the 1880s. The Atchison, Topeka and Sante Fe was one of the most famous American lines, steaming along the romantic Sante Fe trail. The commemorative booklet, right, was published during World War II.

Send Your Wife and Children

YOU may not be able to get away, but is there any good reason why you should not send your wife and children to California for a couple of months?

Think what they would escape — cold and snow and slush and all the other discomforts of a winter in the North.

Think, also, what they would have — sunshine, sea-bathing, flowers, fresh fruits, walks, drives, outdoor life all day and every day.

The train to take is the

Golden State Limited

In service daily, December 20 to April 14, Chicago and Kansas City to Los Angeles, Pasadena, Santa Barbara and San Francisco, via the Rock Island, El Paso-Northeastern and Southern Pacific Systems. Less than three days on the way. Fast as the fastest! Finer than the finest! Compartment and standard sleepers; diner; buffet-smoking-library and observation cars. Lighted by electricity.

Tickets, berths and California literature at any railroad ticket office, or by addressing

JOHN SEBASTIAN,
Passenger Traffic Manager,
CHICAGO, ILL

In the spring of 1878, the Central Pacific Railroad installed a line of telephones through the Sierra Nevada Mountains, in California, to enable track-walkers to report to headquarters at Blue Canyon. In 1879, the first set of telephones equipped with transmitters, receivers and call bells was used for train dispatching by the 9-mile narrow-gauge Boston, Revere Beach & Lynn Railroad. The first known use of the telephone for train dispatching in standard-gauge railway operations was on the Ravena-Schenectady branch of the New York, West Shore & Buffalo Railroad (later part of the New York Central) in January, 1882. Before that happened, however, there was still much railroad history to record.

The first locomotive operated west of the Mississippi River--in 1852--was "The Pacific" of the Pacific Railroad in Missouri (later the Missouri Pacific). This woodburning locomotive, also known as "Pacific Number 3," was unloaded at the Pine Street Wharf, in St. Louis, on August 20, 1852. It made its first run on December 1, 1852, from St. Louis to the end of the line at Cheltenham,

a distance of approximately five miles. Regular passenger service was inaugurated eight days later.

(The expansion of the railroads into the west was greatly facilitated by the land policies of the Federal Government. In 1850, the Federal Government owned nearly 1,400,000,000 acres of land, most of it in the west, and most of which could be neither sold nor settled because it lacked transportation. For a generation, the government had tried to dispose of this land, with little success. In the period 1850-1871, following an earlier policy

Opposite, a Rock Island advertisement from 1904. Want to get rid of the wife and kiddies? Ship 'em off to California!

Below, a British postcard depicting the New York Central's world-renowned Twentieth Century Limited.

Next page, a Sante Fe 4-6-2 Pacific type engine used on Death Valley Scotty's famous speed run between Los Angeles and Chicago in 1905. This particular engine was built in 1903 for the Sante Fe by the Baldwin Locomotive Works.

of granting lands to aid canal and wagon road construction, the government instituted a policy of grants of land to railroad companies, made directly or indirectly through the states. The purpose of the grants was to encourage the construction of railroads through undeveloped territory, to attract settlers, to enhance the value of and create a market for the vast tracts of previously unsalable government-owned lands, to increase taxable wealth, and, most important of all, to strenghten and unify the nation.

(Lands were granted to railroads in alternate sections, checkerboard fashion, with the government retaining the sections between. Despite this largess, Federal land grants accounted for only about 8 per cent of the total mileage of railroad line in the country. More than 91 per cent of the railroad mileage was built with no land grants from the government. Total acreage received by railroads from the Federal Government amounted to 131,363,546 acres, the estimated value of which, at the time of transfer, was approximately 94 cents an acre, or $123,000,000. In return for the lands granted, the land-grant railroads, and railroads which competed with them, carried government troops and all government property used for military purposes for one-half of standard rates until October, 1946. Prior to 1941, the land-grant railroads and competing lines also carried government property used for non-military purposes for one-half of established rates. In addition, the land grant railroads, until 1941, carried

Previous page, Sante Fe engine number 1211 used on Death Valley Scotty's famous speed run between Los Angeles and Chicago in 1905. The run took 44 hours and 54 minutes and cost $5,500. This engine, in charge of Conductor G. H. Rhoades and Engineer E. Sears made the run between Las Vegas and Albuquerque in 3 hours and 8 minutes. This particular engine was built in 1903 for the Sante Fe by the Baldwin Locomotive Works. This 4-6-2 Pacific type locomotive was a common type on the Sante Fe system around the turn of the Century.

LAKE SHORE DEPOT, AUBURN, IND.

United States mails for four-fifths of standard rates. In December, 1945, Congress repealed the land-grant rate provisions, effective October 1, 1946.

(In March, 1945, the Interstate Commerce Committee of the House of Representatives reported that the railroads had already "contributed over $900,000,000 in payment of the lands which were transferred to them under the Land Grant Acts." Between the time of that report and the end of land grant deductions in government rates, there were further payments estimated at not less than $350,000,000. Thus the total contributions of the railroads to the government through rate deductions on account of land grants were approximately ten times the value of the lands at the time they were granted to the railroads.

(The first federal railroad land grant, approved September 20, 1850, conveyed to the State of Illinois 2,595,133 acres of lands which had been on the market for years without purchasers. The price was pegged at $1.25 an acre. The State of Illinois then transferred the lands to the Illinois

Central Railroad Company on condition that the railroad, when completed, would pay the state a charter tax based on a percentage of its gross revenues (in lieu of other taxes) on its 705.5 miles of land-grant railroad in the State, and that it would carry United States troops, property and mails at reduced rates.

(To the end of 1947, the Illinois Central allowed the Federal Government about $24,000,000 in reduced rates on government troops, freight, express and mails, on account of the land grant, and had paid the State of Illinois approximately $117,000,000 in gross revenue tax. It was estimated that the latter was about

Below, an unusual turn of the Century locomotive featuring vertical pistons that served the Tamalpais Scenic Railway in California.

Next Page, the Denver and Rio Grande Railroad ran through some of the most scenic territory in America. This photo, taken around 1920, depicts a 2-8-2 Mikado.

Tamalpais Scenic Ry. on the way to Mt. Tamalpais, Cal.

Twentieth Century Limited leaving Chicago

$47,000,000 greater than normal railway taxes would have been. Thus, to the end of 1947, the raiload had paid some $71,000,000 for lands which could have been purchased outright at the time they were granted for not more than $3,248,000.

(In addition, the Federal Government made loans of bonds to hasten the construction of six pioneer railroads. These were not gifts but were loans, bearing interest at 6 per cent. The amount loaned totalled $64,623,512. The amount repaid, principal and interest, was $167,746,490. In large part owing to the Federal Government's enlightened land and bond policies, the railroads in this fashion expanded rapidly in the west.)

The Sacramento Valley Railroad--"the Days of Gold Railroad"--was formally opened on February 22, 1856, from Sacramento to Folsom, a distance of 22 miles. The locomotives "Sacramento" and "Nevada," which had been shipped around Cape Horn by sailing vessel and barged up the Sacramento River from San Francisco, made their historic runs from Sacramento to Folsom on that date. This railroad later became a part of the

Above, the New York Central's famous Twentieth Century Limited leaving Chicago. This train was for years the fastest scheduled passenger train in the world and regularly made the New York to Chicago run in 18 hours.

Placerville Branch of the Southern Pacific System.

The famous Western scout and Indian fighter, William F. Cody, earned the picturesque nickname of "Buffalo Bill" as a result of his contract to supply buffalo meat in 1867-1868 to the construction forces engaged in building the Kansas Pacific (later part of the Union Pacific Railroad). They needed 12 buffaloes a day, and he took the job for $500 a month. (That worked out to about $1.39 per buffalo, a pretty good deal even in 1867.)

Trains crossing the Western plains in pioneer days were frequently delayed by "thundering herds of buffaloes." In October, 1872, P.T. Barnum, traveling to Denver over the Kansas Pacific with two friends, reported "seeing many thousands of wild buffalo--our train sometimes being stopped to let them pass."

During the construction of the Union Pacific Railroad across the Western Plains and through the Rocky Mountains, temporary towns sprang up almost overnight as the grading, track-laying and bridge gangs advanced westward. The construction forces sometimes consisted of thousands of men and they were usually escorted by companies of armed soldiers for protection against hostile Indians and outlaws, and to maintain order. Restaurant and saloon keepers, gamblers and opportunists of every sex and grade made up this "Hell-on-Wheels," as such migratory towns were most aptly called.

The spanning of the continent by rail occurred barely 40 years after the first successful steam locomotive, the Tom Thumb. This historic event occurred at Promontory, Utah, on May 10, 1869, when the last rails of the Union Pacific and the Central Pacific (later the Southern Pacific) were laid and the tracks were joined to form the first railway line to the Pacific. Spikes of California gold and Nevada silver were driven by distinguished officials. A contemporary account reported:

"When the last spike was driven, the blows of the sledge, as well as the speeches marking the occasion, were carried to the East by telegraph. All over the country whistles were blown, bells were rung, guns were fired, processions were formed, and speeches became the order of the day. Congratulations were showered upon officials of the successful companies. Editors joined in a paean of praise. In truth, the completion of the first transcontinental road marked an epoch!"

The original Golden Spike was subsequently retired to a bank vault in San Francisco. The first railway train ever operated from the Atlantic to the Pacific was the Trans-Continental Excursion sponsored by the Boston Board of Trade in May, 1870, one year after the Union Pacific and Central Pacific railroads were opened. The trip from Boston to San Francisco took eight days and was made in

Below, Sante Fe locomotive number 3000, a Mallett-Articulated compound type built in the Sante Fe shops and, at the time, the largest locomotive in the world.

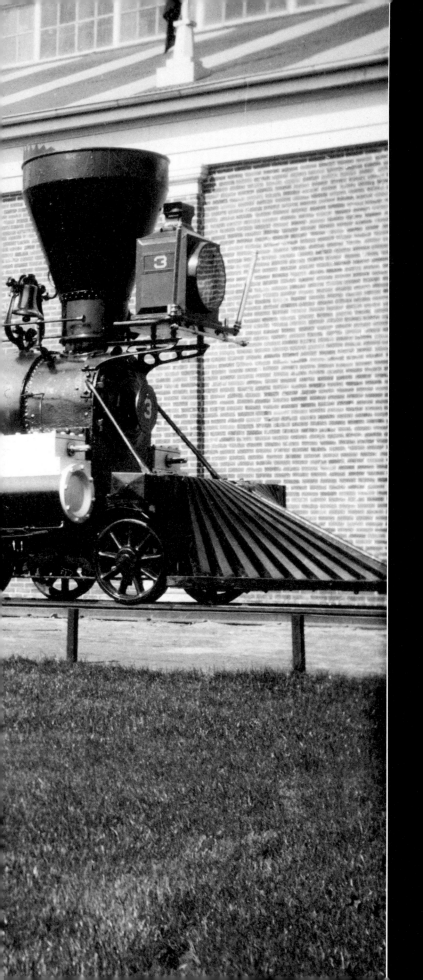

The Famous Chase of the "General"

The "General" was undoubtedly the most famous locomotive of the Civil War--perhaps of the whole of the 19th Century. Belonging to the Western & Atlantic Railroad (later to become part of the Nashville, Chattanooga & St. Louis), the General was a 4-4-0 American type locomotive originally purchased by the line in December, 1855 for $8,500 from Rogers, Ketchum and Grosvenor.

The General was captured at Big Shanty, Georgia, on the morning of April 12, 1862, by Captain James J. Andrews leading a group of 21 Union raiders for the purpose of destroying the railroad and disrupting Confederate supply lines. They first boarded the train at Marietta, Georgia disguised as passengers on their way--so they said-- to join the Confederate Army at Chattanooga.

Eight miles west of Marietta, the train was stopped so the passengers could have breakfast at the Big Shanty Hotel and the raiders made their move. While Captain W. A. Fuller, the conductor and the other passengers were dining, the train suddenly took off without them!

The General was immediately pursued by the Confederates under Captain Fuller, first in a small hand car and later, from Etowah, Georgia in the old engine "Yonah." The General was racing along at speeds of up to 60 miles an hour and the aging Yonah couldn't keep up, so Fuller commandeered another locomotive, the "Shorter," and, later, the "Texas." During the chase, nearly all the General's cars were cut loose to delay the pursuers. Finally, near Ringgold, Georgia just south of Chattanooga, the General ran out of firewood and was abandoned by the raiders. The locomotive was recaptured by Fuller, who pushed it into Ringgold and organized a party of militia to continue the pursuit. All 22 raiders were eventually captured and six, including Andrews, were executed as spies. They later posthumously received the Congressional Medal of Honor.

Previous page, Long Island Railroad's engine number 58. It was photographed at Morris Park in 1903.

Above, a 4-6-2 Pacific on a fast run.

Pullman "hotel cars." A daily newspaper, the"Trans-Continental," was published en route. The Union Pacific and the Central Pacific route between Omaha and Sacramento was completed May 10, 1869, and the extension to San Francisco Bay was opened in the same year.

Following the historic achievement of the linking of the coasts by rails, a long list of important linkages quickly ensued. When they had run their course, the entire continent was linked, east to west, north to south, by ribbons of steel.

The Atchison, Topeka & Santa Fe Railroad from Kansas City and the Southern Pacific line from California effected a junction at Deming, New Mexico, in March, 1881. In so doing, they formed the second rail route to the Pacific and the first direct rail route to southern California. The Southern Pacific route from California to New Orleans was completed and formally opened for business on January 15, 1883.

The last spike in the construction of the Northern Pacific Railroad, the pioneer railroad to the Pacific Northwest, was driven in Hell Gate Canyon, at Gold Creek, Montana, on September 8, 1883. The Oregon Short Line and the Oregon Railway & Navigation Company, forming the Union Pacific route to the Pacific Northwest, joined rails at Huntington, Oregon, November 25, 1884. The lines were opened for through traffic on December 1, 1884. The last rail in the construction of the Great Northern Railroad between the Great Lakes and Everett, Washington, on Puget Sound, was laid on January 5, 1893. Through train service was established in July of that year.

The Atchison, Topeka & Santa Fe Railroad completed its own through route from Chicago to California on May 1, 1888. The San Pedro, Los Angeles & Salt Lake Railroad, now the Union Pacific line from Salt Lake City to southern California, was completed May 1, 1905.

The last spike in the building of the Pacific

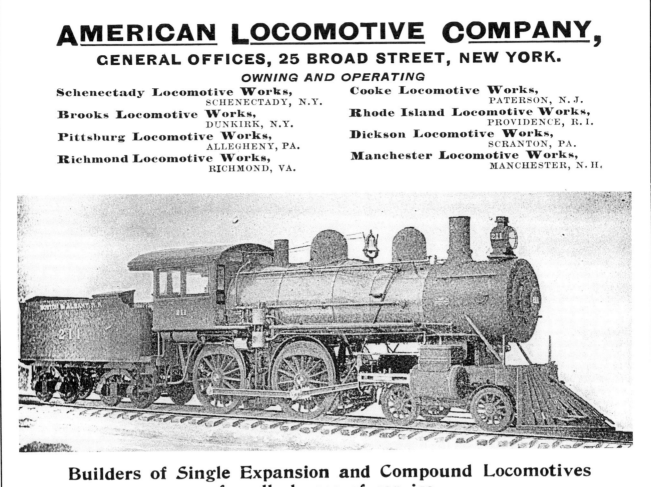
Coast Extension of the Chicago, Milwaukee & St. Paul Railroad (later the Chicago, Milwaukee, St. Paul & Pacific) was driven at Garrison, Montana, May 19, 1909. Through freight service between Chicago and Seattle was established July 4, 1909, and through passenger service was established July 10, 1910.

The Spokane, Portland & Seattle Railway from Spokane to Portland was completed June 10, 1910. The first passenger train to run over the entire line of the Western Pacific Railroad arrived in San Francisco from Salt Lake City on August 22, 1910.

From 1912 to 1935, the Florida East Coast Railway operated trains to and from Key West, over a succession of bridges and viaducts spanning the Florida Keys, and was known as the "Overseas

Above, an ad for the American Locomotive Company (Alco) dating from 1904.

Following page, Wilmington & Western engine number 37, 2-8-2 type, was built in 1924 by Alco (Edward Feathers photo).

Railway." The line was started by Henry Flagler, an original partner of John D. Rockefeller, who later played a key role in developing Florida. In 1935, following a disastrous hurricane which all but destroyed forty miles of track on the Florida Keys, the railway company discontinued train service south of Florida City, thirty miles below Miami. Car ferries which were formerly operated between Key West and Havana, were later operated between New York and New Orleans and Havana.

43

Southern Pacific's new streamline train, the "Daylight", along the scenic Coast Line between Los Angeles and San Francisco.

WORLD'S FASTEST LOCOMOTIVE
Pennsylvania Railroad's No. 7002—Record 127.1 Miles an Hour

Chicago Railroad Fair 1949

Above, Pennsylvania locomotive number 7002. Pulling the Broadway Limited, this engine set the world's record for the fastest run by a railroad train on Monday, June 12, 1905. Near Elida, Ohio, a speed of 127.1 miles per hour was recorded.

Previous pages: Southern Pacific's streamline locomotive speeding along the California coast.

Another car ferry service operated between West Palm Beach, Florida, and Havana.

It was not enough to join the ends of the continent, however. Passengers had to be convinced to use the railroads. To that end, the various rail lines were continually staging speed runs to gain favorable publicity and to demonstrate the convenience of modern rail travel.

In June, 1876, the Jarrett and Palmer Special raced across the country from Jersey City to San Francisco (Oakland Wharf)--a distance of 3,312 miles--in an amazing 84 hours and 20 minutes, or in about three-and-a-half days. Three cars and 19 locomotives were used during the trip.

On July 8, 1905, Walter Scott, a Californian of legendary wealth, better known as "Death Valley Scotty," asked the Santa Fe Railroad in Los Angeles for a special train to take him to Chicago faster than any human being had ever made the trip before. Scott was told that the 2,265-mile trip could be made in forty-six hours at a cost of $5,500. The deal was closed and at 1 p.m. on Sunday, July 9, 1905, Scott's "Coyote Special" left Los Angeles on its history-making run. He arrived at Dearborn Station, Chicago, 44 hours and 54 minutes later, on July 11th at 11:45 a.m. In so doing, he beat the previous record by a remarkable 13 hours and 2 minutes. One of the locomotives used on this run is pictured on pages 30-31.

In the aftermath of the 1906 San Francisco earthquake, the well-known railroad baron, Edward H. Harriman, wanted to return to New York on urgent business. In order to accomplish this, he made the run in a special train from San Francisco to New York--a distance of 3,344 miles--in 71 hours and 27 minutes, the fastest coast-

The New York Central's "Empire State Express" Most Famous Train in the World.

to-coast rail travel time until October, 1934, when the Union Pacific Diesel-powered streamliner "City of Portland" (M-10001) made an experimental run from Los Angeles to New York City--a distance of 3,258 miles--in 56 hours and 55 minutes (including stops en route!). This is the fastest transcontinental passenger run ever made by a single train.

On May 11, 1893, New York Central locomotive No. "999" became the fastest creation of man up to that time, running a mile in 32 seconds (112.5 miles per hour) near Batavia, New York. It was the first 100 mile-per-hour locomotive and, remarkably, held the world's speed record for more than twelve years.

On June 12, 1905, the Pennsylvania Special, later called the Broadway Limited, of the Pennsylvania Railroad, ran three miles in Ohio in 85 seconds. This worked out to a rate of 127.06 miles per hour, a new record and one that still stands for steam locomotives.

There was far more to successful railroading than distance and speed, however. In linking America with rails, the railroads were compelled to exercise remarkable ingenuity in overcoming many obstacles and in satisfying many

Before the Broadway Limited, the Empire State Express of the New York Central was the fastest long-distance train, making the 440 mile trip between New York City and Buffalo in eight-and-a-quarter hours.

needs of both passengers and industry. The development of passenger cars is covered in another chapter, but other railroad achievements are impossible to ignore in a complete examination of the contribution to the nation's advancement of America's railroads in the steam era.

On November 1, 1865, about six years after the world's first oil well was opened at Titusville, Pennsylvania, the first tank car was loaded in that city. It was a flat car fitted with two wooden tanks shaped like inverted tubs. Many of these "rotary" oil cars, as they were called, were used for years transporting oil from the Pennsylvania wells. Ultimately, they were replaced by the modern type of horizontal cylindrical tank, fitted with a dome which allows the oil to expand without injury to the tank. The first tank car of this type was introduced in 1868.

The rails themselves, without which

railroads would be a logical impossibility, underwent their own fascinating process of development. The earliest railroads in the United States were built with wooden rails capped with thin strips, or "straps," of iron to provide a running surface for the wheels of the trains. These were called "straprails." The straprails, however, were inadequate to the requirements of steam trains, most of which were simply too heavy for them to carry successfully. A stronger, more durable type was urgently needed.

Iron rails--18 feet in length--were imported from England as early as 1831. The first iron rails of American design were rolled in the United States in 1844 and, by 1850, most railroads were being built with iron rails.

The first Bessemer steel rails manufactured in the United States were rolled at the North Chicago Rolling Mills on May 25, 1865. By 1880, about 30 per cent of all tracks in the United States were laid with steel rails. Within ten years, 80 per cent of the country's mileage was equipped with steel rails and, by the late 1890s, steel had almost completely replaced iron.

Track gauge was also a major problem to

Above: Early streamlining seen at the Century of Progress Exposition in Chicago. The locomotive is number 653 from the Delaware and Hudson line.

be dealt with in the development of the railroads. Gauge is the space, in feet and inches, between the parallel rails of a track, the gaugeline being measured at a point five-eighths of an inch below the top of the rail. In the United States, and in many foreign countries, the standard gauge is 4 feet 8 1/2 inches.

There has been much speculation and debate as to the origin of the 4-foot 8-1/2-inch gauge. In England, the first successful public railroads were powered by steam locomotives built by George Stephenson, who probably adopted the 4-foot 8-1/2-inch gauge as a result of his experience in building engines for a colliery line which had a gauge of approximately that width. Other English railroads followed Stephenson's example until, by 1846, the majority of them were of the 4-foot 8-1/2-inch gauge. In that year, Parliament settled the gauge question in England by requiring that all future railroads be built to the gauge adopted by

Above, a more advanced example of streamlining than opposite. This is the "Hiawatha" of the Milwaukee Road line.

Stephenson.

The Stephenson gauge was adopted by a number of the railroads in the United States. Nevertheless, many other gauges were also used. During one period of time, from 1865 to 1871, it was possible to travel all the way from New York to St. Louis over railroads with a gauge of six feet--the broadest that ever existed in North America. This line of railroads was aptly known as the "Great Broad Gauge Route."

In 1871, no fewer than twenty-three different gauges, ranging from three feet to six feet, existed on the railroads of the United States, making it impossible for freight or passenger cars to be freely interchanged. As the necessity for such interchange became increasingly apparent, the railroads began a movement for standardization of

gauge. By 1887, virtually every important broad gauge railroad in the United States had changed to 4 feet 8-1/2 inches, which by that time had come to be known as the "standard" gauge.

Of the 225,806 miles of railroad in this country toward the end of the steam era at the end of World War II, 224,948 miles, or 99.6 per cent, were standard gauge lines. Of the remainder, 858 miles were 3-foot narrow gauge lines and 61 miles of railroad tracks were equipped with three rails to accommodate both standard and narrow gauge equipment.

Railroads achieved many heights during their development in the steam era--some of them literally. The highest point reached by a railroad in the United States was the summit of Pike's Peak in Colorado, 14,110 feet above sea level, served by the Manitou & Pikes's Peak (cog) Railway. The highest point reached by a railroad using adhesion or smooth rails (rather than cog or rack rails) was at Climax, Colorado, on the Colorado & Southern

Railway, where the elevation is 11,319 feet above sea level. The Denver & Rio Grande Western Railroad reached elevations of 10,856 feet above sea level at Marshall Pass, Colorado (narrow gauge) and 10,331 feet at Resurrection Mill, Colorado (standard gauge).

Railroads also plumbed the depths. The lowest point reached by a railroad in this country was at milepost 635.4, near Salton, California, where the Southern Pacific Railroad, in crossing the Salton "sink" and the Imperial Valley, reached a depth of 199.2 feet below sea level.

Where going up or down wouldn't work, the railroads could always find a way to go through. By the end of the steam era, there were approximately 1,500 railroad tunnels in the country with an aggregate length of about 320 miles.

The first railroad tunnel in this country was constructed in 1833, four miles east of Johnstown, Pennsylvania, for the Allegheny Portage Railroad (later a part of the Pennsylvania Railroad). The Hoosac Tunnel on the Boston & Maine Railroad under Hoosac Mountain, Massachusetts, was the oldest of the long railway tunnels still in use in this country at the close of the steam era. It was a mammoth undertaking and constituted one of the engineering wonders of the late 19th century. Twenty-five years were required for its construction. The tunnel--4 miles 3,961 feet in length--was commenced in 1851, holed through on November 27, 1873 and completed so as to admit passage of cars on February 9, 1875. It was electrified in 1911 and, alas, completely dieselized by 1946.

The Cascade Tunnel, on the Great Northern Railroad through the Cascade Mountains in Washington State, was 41,152 feet (7.79 miles) in length, and was the longest railroad tunnel in the Western Hemisphere. The Moffat Tunnel, of the Denver & Rio Grande Western Railroad (under James Peak in Colorado) was 6 miles 1,118 feet in length, and was the second longest railroad tunnel in the United States.

The shortest railroad tunnel in this country during the steam era was the Bee Rock Tunnel--a

Below, the Pennsylvania's Broadway Limited as advertised in the 1920's.

mere 30 feet in length--on the Louisville and Nashville Railroad near Apalachia, Virginia. It was, in fact, said to be the smallest in the world.

The Natural Tunnel, on the Southern Railway, in southwest Virginia, was believed to be the only natural tunnel in the world used by a railroad. It was 100 feet high, 100 to 175 feet wide, and 1,557 feet in length.

Geographical obstacles that could not be crossed or penetrated could be spanned. By the close of the steam era, there were approximately 191,800 railroad bridges (with an aggregate length of 3,860 miles) in the railway structure of the United States.

The first iron railroad bridge in the United States is believed to have been built for the Reading Railroad in 1845 near Manayunk, Pennsylvania. The Rock Island Railroad bridge at Davenport, Iowa, opened in 1856, was the first to span the Mississippi River. Built of wood and resting on stone piers, this 1,582 foot structure was described as "the mechanical wonder of the West." The locomotive "Des Moines" was the first to cross the bridge, on April 21, 1856. The first all-steel railway

bridge was a 2,700-ft. structure completed at Glasgow, Missouri, in 1879, for the Chicago & Alton (later a part of the Gulf, Mobile & Ohio).

The 12-mile pile-trestle bridge carrying the tracks of the Southern Pacific Railroad across Great Salt Lake in Utah was the longest steam era railway bridge structure in the United States. Completed in 1903, it formed a part of the Lucin Cut-off..

The Huey Long Bridge, 4.4 miles in length including approaches, across the Mississippi River above New Orleans, was the longest steam era railway-highway bridge built of steel and concrete construction in the United States. It was opened in December, 1935, and used by the Southern Pacific, Missouri Pacific and Texas & Pacific railroads.

By the end of World War II, there were approximately 46,000 locomotives of all types in use in the United States. Of these, about 85 percent were steam-driven. Despite these seemingly overwhelming numbers, the era of the steam locomotive was nearly at an end. Within a generation, the steam locomotive was to become all but a memory, treasured and kept alive in America by a dedicated group of steam railroad enthusiasts.

Development of Steam Railroad Transportation in the United States

On the following pages are maps defining in graphic terms the incredible growth of the American railroads in the steam era. In a sense, the railroads mirrored the growth of the nation from an essentially coastal one located along the eastern seaboard to the great continent-embracing nation of today. In a larger sense, however, the role of the steam railroads in spurring that growth--indeed, in making it possible--should not be overlooked.

Between 1830 and 1840, completed rail lines increased from 23 to 2,818 miles. During the next decade, that figure rose to 6,200 miles. By 1850, one could travel all the way from Boston to Wilmington, North Carolina by rail. The railroads

were still concentrated along the Atlantic coast, but that was soon to change.

By 1860, the railroads were rapidly expanding westward to the Mississippi and beyond. At the outbreak of the Civil War, a grand total of 30,626 miles of track existed. Although the war halted construction for a time, lineage rose to 52,922 miles by 1870 and it was during this decade that the continent was joined with the first transcontinental railroad.

The total track mileage increased again to 93,296 miles by 1880 and to 163,597 miles by 1890. By the end of World War II, lineage stood at 226,000 miles.

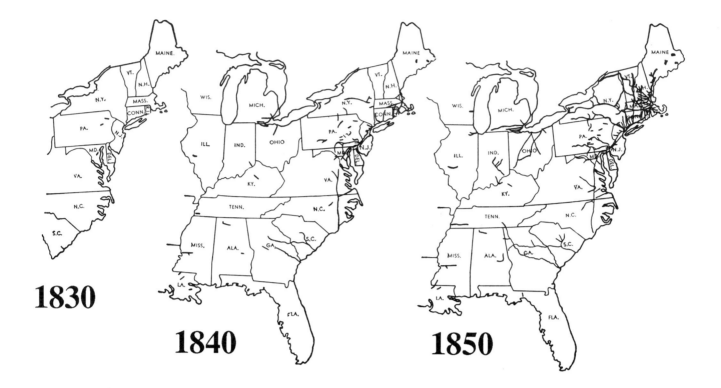

1830

1840

1850

1860

1870

1880

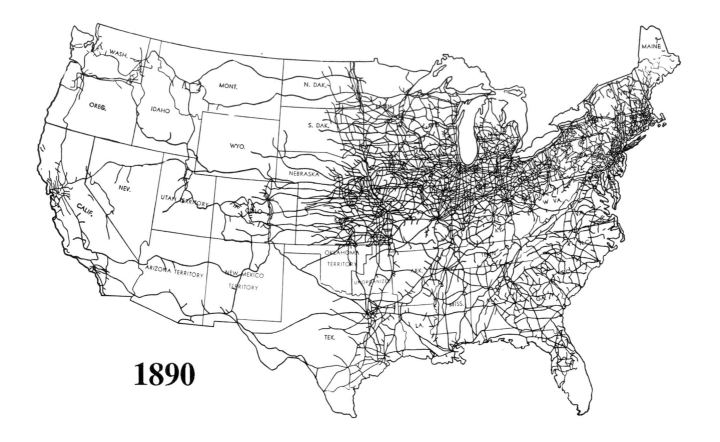

1890

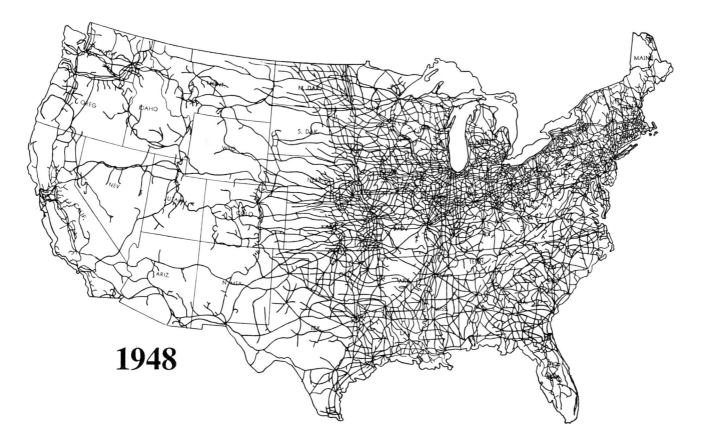

1948

CHAPTER TWO

The Last of the American Steam Locomotives

As has been the case in many fields throughout history, the peak of steam locomotive technology was reached after new types of

Previous page: Among the most advanced of all streamline locomotives was the Pennsylvania Railroad's T-1 series. The weight of this engine (including tender) was 930,000 pounds and it had a tractive force of 64,650 pounds. It was truly a giant among giants. This art (which also graces our cover) formed the other half of the ad that appears on page 8.

technology had made it obsolete. In the 1930s and 1940s, when the advent of the diesel locomotive and the airplane had rendered the demise of the steam locomotive virtually certain, steam engines of staggering size, power and beauty were built in the railroad shops of America.

The American Locomotive Company was one of the greatest of the builders of steam locomotives in this country throughout the steam era. Reproduced on the following pages are seven of their later steam locomotives spanning the period from 1928 to 1940. A wide variety of locomotive

types is represented, including Challenger, Atlantic, Texas, Northern and Berkshire. This group includes the famous streamlined "Hiawatha" of the Milwaukee Road.

The next group of locomotives is from the Pennsylvania system, the photos and specifications dating from 1944. The Pennsylvania Railroad was not only the largest line in the country, it ran some of the largest and most technologically advanced steam locomotives ever built anywhere in the world.

These include the fabulous "S" and "T" types, some of which featured turbine direct-drive which did away with the traditional cylinder-drive that had powered steam locomotives since the earliest days.

The final group of steam locomotives includes several from the Norfolk and Western system in the late 1940s. The Norfolk and Western, incidentally, made steam era history when it took delivery of the very last steam locomotive in America, an 0-8-0 switcher, in 1953.

AMERICAN LOCOMOTIVE COMPANY
NEW YORK

Class, 284 S 404   Road Number, 1125

BUILT FOR THE MISSOURI PACIFIC.

GAUGE OF TRACK	CYLINDERS		DRIVING WHEEL DIAMETER	BOILER		FIRE BOX		TUBES		
	Diameter	Stroke		Inside Dia.	Pressure	Length	Width	Number	Diameter	Length
4'-8½"	28"	30"	63"	86"	240 lbs.	150⅛"	96¼"	84 204	2¼" 3½"	20'-0"

WHEEL BASE			WEIGHT IN WORKING ORDER—POUNDS						
Driving	Engine	Engine & Tender	Leading	Driving	Trailing		Engine	Tender	
					FRONT	REAR			
16'-9"	39'-8"	84'-9½"	34500	267500	41500	60500	404000	285600	

FUEL	EVAPORATING SURFACES, SQUARE FT						SUPERHEATING SURFACE SQUARE FT.	GRATE AREA SQ. FT.	MAXIMUM TRACTIVE POWER		FACTOR OF ADHESION	
Kind	Tubes	Flues	Fire Box	Arch Tubes	Syphons	Total			Engine 61.8 % Cut-off	BOOSTER 80% Cut off	Drivers	Trailer
Soft Coal	984	3719	291	21	103	5118	2121	100.3	70500 lbs.	13200 lbs.	3.79	4.58

Tender Type, 12-Wheeled   Capacity, Water, 15000 Gals.   Fuel, 18 Tons.

ORDER No. S-1624
December, 1928

AMERICAN LOCOMOTIVE COMPANY
NEW YORK

1936 + 1937

Class, 442 S 280

Road Number, 1

BUILT FOR THE C. M. ST. P. & P. R. R.

GAUGE OF TRACK	CYLINDERS		DRIVING WHEEL DIAMETER	BOILER		FIRE BOX		TUBES		
	Diam.	Stroke		Inside Dia.	Pressure	Length	Width	Number	Diameter	Length
4'-8½"	19"	28"	84"	76¹¹⁄₁₆"	300 lbs.	132¹⁄₁₆"	75³⁄₁₆"	160 43	2¼" 5½"	19'-0"

WHEEL BASE			WEIGHT IN WORKING ORDER – POUNDS				
Driving	Engine	Engine & Tender	Leading	Driving	Trailing	Engine	Tender
8'-6"	37'-7"	78'-10½"	75000	140000	65000	280000	247500

FUEL	EVAPORATING SURFACES, SQUARE FT.					SUPERHEATING SURFACE SQUARE FT.	GRATE AREA SQ. FT.	MAXIMUM TRACTIVE POWER	FACTOR OF ADHESION
Kind	Tubes	Flues	Fire Box	Syphon	Total				
Oil	1781	1170	254	40	3245	1029	69	30700 lbs.	4.56

Tender Type. 10-Wheeled

Capacity, Water, 13000 Gals.

Fuel, 4000 Gals

Approx H.P. AT. 80 M.P.H.
DRAW BAR PULL OF 8 CARS.

ORDER No. S-1740
April, 1935

60

AMERICAN LOCOMOTIVE COMPANY
NEW YORK

Class, 2104 S 419   Road Number, 702

BUILT FOR THE CENTRAL VERMONT.

GAUGE OF TRACK	CYLINDERS		DRIVING WHEEL DIAMETER	BOILER		FIRE BOX		TUBES		
	Diameter	Stroke		Inside Dia.	Pressure	Length	Width	Number	Diameter	Length
4'-8½"	27"	32"	60"	84½"	250 lbs.	126⅛"	96¼"	33 192	2¼" 3½"	22'-0"

WHEEL BASE			WEIGHT IN WORKING ORDER—POUNDS					
Driving	Engine	Engine & Tender	Leading	Driving	Trailing FRONT	REAR	Engine	Tender
22'-0"	44'-2"	82'-2¼"	35000	285000	44500	54500	419000	269600

FUEL	EVAPORATING SURFACES, SQUARE FT						SUPERHEATING SURFACE SQUARE FT.	GRATE AREA SQ. FT.	MAXIMUM TRACTIVE POWER		FACTOR OF ADHESION	
Kind	Tubes	Flues	Fire Box	Arch Tubes	Syphons	Total			Engine 62.6 % Cut-off	BOOSTER 50% Cut-off	Drivers	Trailer
Soft Coal	426	3854	321	22	80	4703	2208	84.4	76800 lbs.	13100 lbs.	3.71	4.16

Tender Type, 12-Wheeled   Capacity, Water, 13500 Gals.   Fuel, 20 Tons.

ORDER No. S-1630
October, 1928

AMERICAN LOCOMOTIVE COMPANY
NEW YORK

Class, 484 S 418   Road Number, 1111

BUILT FOR THE TIMKEN ROLLER BEARING CO.

GAUGE OF TRACK	CYLINDERS		DRIVING WHEEL DIAMETER	BOILER		FIRE BOX		TUBES		
	Diameter	Stroke		Inside Dia.	Pressure	Length	Width	Number	Diameter	Length
4'-8½"	27"	30"	73"	84¼"	235 250	132⅛"	96¼"	66 194	2¼" 3½"	21'-6"

WHEEL BASE			WEIGHT IN WORKING ORDER—POUNDS					
Driving	Engine	Engine & Tender	Leading	Driving	Trailing		Engine	Tender
					FRONT	REAR		
19'-3"	45'-10"	89'-9¼"	67500 58500	246000 264000	48500 44000	55500 51000	417500	294000

FUEL	EVAPORATING SURFACES, SQUARE FT						SUPERHEATING SURFACE SQUARE FT.	GRATE AREA SQ. FT.	MAXIMUM TRACTIVE POWER		FACTOR OF ADHESION	
Kind	Tubes	Flués	Fire Box	Arch Tubes	Syphons	Total			Engine	Booster	Drivers	Trailer
Soft Coal	832	3805	360	18	105	5120	2157	88.3	59900 63700	12000 12800	4.10 4.14	4.62 4.00

Tender Type, 12-Wheeled   Capacity, Water, 14200 Gals.   Fuel, 21 Tons.

ORDER No. S-1665
April, 1930

AMERICAN LOCOMOTIVE COMPANY
NEW YORK

Class, 484 S 436   Road Number, 5027

BUILT FOR THE CHICAGO ROCK ISLAND & PACIFIC.

GAUGE OF TRACK	CYLINDERS		DRIVING WHEEL DIAMETER	BOILER		FIRE BOX		TUBES		
	Diameter	Stroke		Inside Dia.	Pressure	Length	Width	Number	Diameter	Length
4'-8½"	26"	32"	69"	84¼"	250 lbs	132⅛"	96¼"	77 202	2¼" 3½"	21'-6"

WHEEL BASE			WEIGHT IN WORKING ORDER—POUNDS					
Driving	Engine	Engine & Tender	Leading	Driving	Trailing		Engine	Tender
					FRONT	REAR		
19'-3"	45'-7"	88'-0"	69000	266500	43000	57500	436000	304300

FUEL	EVAPORATING SURFACES, SQUARE FT					SUPERHEATING SURFACE SQUARE FT.	GRATE AREA SQ. FT.	MAXIMUM TRACTIVE POWER		FACTOR OF ADHESION	
Kind	Tubes	Flues	Fire Box	Syphons	Total			Engine 82% Cut-off	BOOSTER 50% Cut-off	Drivers	Trailer
Soft Coal	970	3958	364	151	5443	2243	88.3	66000 lbs.	13100 lbs.	4.03	4.38

Tender Type, 12-Wheeled   Capacity, Water, 15000 Gals.   Fuel, 20 Tons.

ORDER No. S-1686
March, 1930

AMERICAN LOCOMOTIVE COMPANY
NEW YORK

Class, "Four Cylinder Simple" 4664 S 625

Nov. 1936.

Road Number, 5107

BUILT FOR THE NORTHERN PACIFIC.

GAUGE OF TRACK	CYLINDERS		DRIVING WHEEL DIAMETER	BOILER		FIRE BOX		TUBES		
	Diam.	Stroke		Inside Dia.	Pressure	GAINES ARCH		Number	Diameter	Length
						Length	Width			
4'-8½"	23"	32"	69"	96⅜"	250 lbs.	246⅛"	114¼"	192 / 73	2¼" / 5½"	23'-0"

WHEEL BASE			WEIGHT IN WORKING ORDER—POUNDS				
Driving	Engine	Engine & Tender	Leading	Driving	Trailing	Engine	Tender
12'-2" & 12'-2"	61'-10"	113'-8"	73000	435000	116500	624500	398500

FUEL	EVAPORATING SURFACES. SQUARE FT.					SUPERHEATING SURFACE SQUARE FT.	GRATE		MAXIMUM TRACTIVE POWER	FACTOR OF ADHESION
Kind	Tubes	Flues	Fire Box	Syphons	Total		Length	Width		
							192"	114¼"		
Rosebud Coal	2589	2405	626	213	5832	2114	152.3 Sq.Ft.		104500 lbs.	4.16

Tender Type, 12 Wheeled   Capacity, Water, 20000 Gals.   Fuel, 27 Tons.

ORDER No. S-1758
December, 1936

HORSE POWER

AMERICAN LOCOMOTIVE COMPANY
NEW YORK

Class, "Four Cylinder Simple" 4664 S 597   Road Number, 1505
BUILT FOR THE DELAWARE & HUDSON RAILROAD CORPORATION.

GAUGE OF TRACK	CYLINDERS		DRIVING WHEEL DIAMETER	BOILER		FIRE BOX		TUBES		
	Diam.	Stroke		Inside Dia.	Pressure	GAINES ARCH		Number	Diameter	Length
						Length	Width			
4'-8½"	20½"	32"	69"	94¹¹⁄₁₆"	285 lbs.	213¹⁄₃₂"	108³⁄₁₆"	222 60	2¼" 5½"	22'-0"

WHEEL BASE			WEIGHT IN WORKING ORDER POUNDS				
Driving	Engine	Engine & Tender	Leading	Driving	Trailing	Engine	Tender (⅔ Load)
12'-2" & 12'-2"	59'-11"	103'-6"	76000	406500	114500	597000	310200

FUEL	EVAPORATING SURFACES. SQ. FT.					SUPERHEATING SURFACE SQUARE FT.	GRATE		MAXIMUM TRACTIVE POWER	FACTOR OF ADHESION
Kind	Tubes	Flues	Fire Box	Arch Tubes	Total		Length 143²³⁄₃₂"	Width 108³⁄₁₆"		
Soft Coal	2864	1892	556	77	5389	1681	108 Sq. Ft		94400 lbs.	4.31

Tender Type 12-Wheeled   Capacity, Water, 22500 Gals   Fuel, 26 Tons
ORDER No. S-1824
July, 1940

As is the case with any huge industry, huge sums were regularly spent by the railroad companies on research of various kinds. The dramatic changes in steam locomotive technology illustrated in this book are ample proof that American railroads worked hard at perfecting in every way possible steam locomotive. They kept in the van of technological progress, not only by constantly engaging in original work of their own, but also by diligently following the development of every branch of science and engineering for discoveries and advances adaptable to railroad use. That the onrush of progress ultimately dictated the demise of the steam locomotive itself is a fact regretted by steam buffs the world over. Still, some consolation can be taken in the fact that the last steam engines were in many cases fabulous, indeed.

The Pennsylvania Railroad was more loyal than most lines to the steam engine. This loyalty was influenced by the fact that bituminous coal was (and is) abundantly available in high quality in the home territory of that road.

In the early 1940s, the Penn system introduced the first direct drive steam turbine locomotive ever built in the United States. Designated the S-2, this coal-burning steam locomotive differed from locomotives of conventional design in that it was powered by a turbine instead of by reciprocating engines. In that, it was the first direct drive steam turbine locomotive ever built in the United States and was intended to serve the Pennsylvania systems's long-distance high-speed passenger and freight service.

In the S-2, the turbine shaft was rotated by the pressure of jets of steam against the blades of the turbine wheel, and a continuous flow of power was transmitted to the driving wheels through speed reducing gears. The engine was designed and constructed by the Baldwin Locomotive Works and the Westinghouse Electric and Manufacturing Company, in collaboration with the Pennsylvania Railroad.

The idea behind the development of the S-2 steam turbine locomotive was to eliminate the reciprocating parts of the conventional steam engine, obtain a uniform flow of power to the driving wheels, and secure the significant economies inherent in a turbine for railroad motive power. The turbine was designed to develop 6,900 shaft horsepower, and provide power sufficient to pull a full-length passenger train at speeds of up to 100 miles per hour.

The S-2 engine featured remarkably simple operation. Both forward and reverse movements, at all speeds, were controlled by a single lever, actuating specially designed pneumatic control apparatus. Automatically functioning devices were designed to render, as nearly as humanly possible, incorrect handling of the mechanism impossible.

Accounting for less than 1 percent of the engine's total weight, the main--or forward drive--turbine was mounted at the right hand side of the locomotive. A smaller turbine, designed to move the locomotive backward at speeds up to 22 miles an hour, was mounted on the left side, and was brought into operation through the simple engagement of a clutch.

The forward turbine featured more than 1,000 chromium steel blades, some of which were less than one inch in length. Steam traveled through the entire battery of turbine blades, expending all of its energy except approximately 15 pounds, in the process producing a non-pulsating draft through the firebox and boiler. The boiler itself was of a conventional type, carrying 310 pounds of steam pressure and fired by mechanical stoker.

The heat-treated alloy steel reducing gears, into which the turbine shaft fed its power, operated continuously in an oil bath and meshed with so little friction that, under optimum conditions, as much as 97 per cent of the turbine's power reached the driving wheels. Power was applied directly to two center pairs of driving wheels and transmitted to two additional pairs of drivers by connecting rods. The engine, with its 6-8-6 wheel arrangement, was equipped with roller bearings throughout.

While the S-2 was undergoing prototype testing, the Pennsylvania Railroad's newest four-cylinder coal-burning steam passenger locomotive in regular service--designated Class T-1--was being operated at speeds up to 120 miles an hour at the road's test plant at Altoona, Pennsylvania. By

1944, two locomotives of this type were already in service on the railroad's fastest passenger trains.

The T-1 was in many ways typical of the multiple-cylinder coal-burning steam locomotives the Pennsylvania Railroad had been developing for several years, having produced, in addition to the T-1, the S-1, the world's largest and fastest passenger steam locomotive and the related Q-1 and Q-2 freight locomotives.

The Pennsylvania Railroad's S-1 coal-burning steam passenger locomotive was the streamlined monster of America's railroads in the mid-1940s. It measured 140 feet, 2-1/2 inches, from the pulling face of the pilot coupler to the pulling face of the tender coupler, and not only was the largest passenger engine in the world, but the fastest. The S-1 was the first four-cylinder engine to be built in the Pennsylvania's wartime-era program of developing multiple-cylinder engines.

The Q-2 was placed under production during the summer of 1944 by the Pennsylvania at its Altoona Works and 25 were constructed on the first order. This locomotive was capable of pulling a train of 125 loaded freight cars at speeds in excess of 50 miles an hour.

The Q-2 engine was designed to develop more power in its working range (at speeds over 20 miles an hour) than any steam locomotive ever built up to that time. It was designed to speed the movement of freight in two ways: first by moving heavier trains with increased speeds and, second, by making longer continuous runs without stopping for coal, thus cutting down time materially increasing over-all train speeds.

More common in 1944 were the Pennsylvania's large fleet of Class J-1 coal-burning steam freight locomotives. They were built to assist in the prompt movement of war-time freight.

The M-1a was another coal-burning freight locomotive performing fast freight service. It also did an efficient job on heavy through passenger runs when needed. The K-4s coal-burning passenger locomotive, running in high-speed passenger service, also pulled some of the Pennsylvnia Railroad's most famous trains. The railroad maintained large fleets of both M-1a and K-4s engines.

Below: An artist's rendering of the Pennsylvania Railroad's Q-2 Class advanced steam locomotive.

Pennsylvania Class S-2

Length overall, from coupler face to coupler face, 122 feet, 7-1/4 inches. Height, 16 feet.
Steam Turbine, Direct Drive (No Cylinders).Steam Pressure, 310 pounds per square inch.
Driving Wheel Diameter, 68 inches.Wheel Arrangement, 6-8-6.Weight on Driving Wheels, 260,000
pounds.Total Weight of Locomotive and Tender in Working Order, 1,032,100 pounds.
Tractive Effort, 65,000 pounds.Capacity of Tender, 85,000 pounds of Coal, 19,500 gallons of Water.

Pennsylvania Class T-1

Length overall, from coupler face to coupler face, 122 feet, 9-3/4inches. Height, 15 feet, 6 inches.
Cylinders, 19-3/4-inch diameter, 26-inch stroke. Steam Pressure, 300 pounds per square inch. Driving
Wheel Diameter, 80 inches.Wheel Arrangement 4-4-4-4.
Weight on Driving Wheels, 268,200 pounds. Total Weight of Locomotive and Tender in Working Order,
930,200 pounds.Tractive Effort, 64,650 pounds.Capacity of Tender, 82,000 pounds of Coal, 19,500 gallons
of Water.

Pennsylvania Class Q-2

Length overall, from coupler face to coupler face, 124 feet, 7-1/8 inches.
Height, 16 feet, 5-1/2 inches.Cylinders, Front--19-3/4 inch diameter, 28-inch stroke. Rear--23-3/4 inch diameter, 29-inch stroke. Steam Pressure, 300 pounds per square inch.
Driving Wheel Diameter, 69 inches.Wheel Arrangement 4-4-6-4.Weight on Driving Wheels, 388,400 pounds.Total Weight of Locomotive and Tender in Working Order, 1,053,100 pounds.
Tractive Effort, 99,860 pounds (with Booster, 114,860 pounds).Capacity of Tender, 79,700 pounds of Coal, 19,020 gallons of Water.

Pennsylvania Class S-1

Length overall, from coupler face to coupler face, 140 feet, 2-1/2 inches-Height, 15 feet, 6 inches.
Cylinders, 22-inch diameter, 26-inch stroke. Steam Pressure 300 pounds per square inch. Driving Wheel Diameter, 84 inches.Wheel Arrangement 6-4-4-6.Weight on Driving Wheels, 281,440 pounds. Total Weight of Locomotive and Tender in Working Order, 1,060,010 pounds. Tractive Effort, 71,900 pounds.Capacity of Tender, 52,900 pounds of Coal, 24,230 gallons of Water.

Pennsylvania Class Q-1

Length overall, from coupler face to coupler face, 122 feet, 9-3/4 inches. Height, 15 feet, 6 inches.
Cylinders, Front--23-inch diameter, 28-inch stroke. Rear--19-1/2-inch diameter,
26-inch stroke. Steam Pressure, 300 pounds per square inch. Driving Wheel Diameter, 77 inches. Wheel
Arrangement 4-6-4-4.Weight on Driving Wheels, 354,700 pounds.
Total Weight of Locomotive and Tender in Working Order, 1,027,870 pounds. Tractive Effort, 81,793
pounds (w/Booster, 93,043 pounds). Capacity of Tender, 82,640 pounds of Coal, 19,167 gallons of Water.

Pennsylvania Class J-1

Length overall, from coupler face to coupler face, 117 feet, 8 inches. Height, 16 feet, 5-1/2 inches.
Cylinders, 29-inch diameter, 34-inch stroke. Steam Pressure, 270 pounds per square inch. Driving Wheel
Diameter, 69 inches. Wheel Arrangement 2-10-4. Weight on Driving Wheels, 379,493 pounds. Total
Weight of Locomotive and Tender in Working Order, 987,380 pounds. Tractive Effort, 95,100 pounds
(With Booster, 110,100 pounds).Capacity of Tender, 59,800 pounds of Coal, 21,000 gallons of Water.

Pennsylvania Class K-4s

Length overall, from coupler face to coupler face, 83 feet. Height, 15 feet. Cylinders, 27-inch diameter, 28-inch stroke. Steam Pressure, 205 pounds per square inch. Driving Wheel Diameter, 80 inches. Wheel Arrangement 4-6-2.Weight on Driving Wheels, 209,300 pounds.
Total Weight of Locomotive and Tender in Working Order, 541,500 pounds.Tractive Effort, 44,460 pounds. Capacity of Tender, 43,600 pounds of Coal, 11,300 gallons of Water.

Pennsylvania Class M-1a

Length overall, from coupler face to coupler face, 108 feet, 2-3/8 inches. Height, 15 feet, 6 inches. Cylinders, 27-inch diameter, 30-inch stroke.Steam Pressure, 250 pounds. Driving Wheel Diameter, 72 inches.Wheel Arrangement 4-8-2. Weight on Driving Wheels, 271,000 pounds. Total Weight of Locomotive and Tender in Working Order, 768,360 pounds. Tractive Effort, 64,550 pounds. Capacity of Tender, 63,000 pounds of Coal, 222,090 gallons of Water.

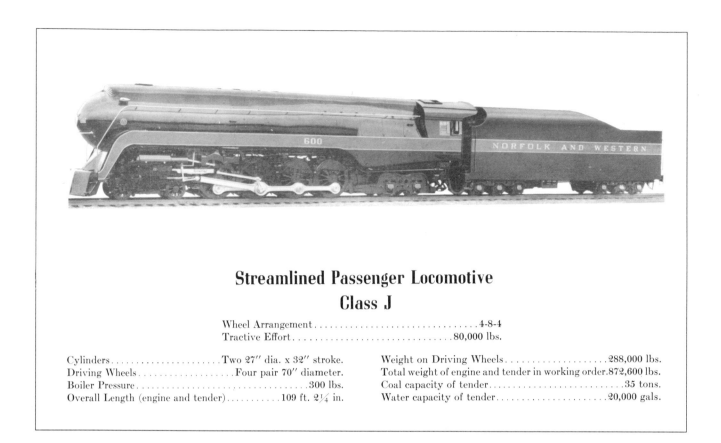

Streamlined Passenger Locomotive
Class J

Wheel Arrangement................................4-8-4
Tractive Effort............................80,000 lbs.

Cylinders....................Two 27″ dia. x 32″ stroke.
Driving Wheels.................Four pair 70″ diameter.
Boiler Pressure................................300 lbs.
Overall Length (engine and tender)..........109 ft. 2¼ in.

Weight on Driving Wheels...................288,000 lbs.
Total weight of engine and tender in working order.872,600 lbs.
Coal capacity of tender..........................35 tons.
Water capacity of tender....................20,000 gals.

In 1953, the Norfolk and Western took delivery of the very last steam locomotive on any American railroad. In fact, during the final years of the steam era, the Norfolk and Western Railway designed and constructed more than 100 modern steam locomotives. By the term "modern steam locomotive" was meant a locomotive designed with a high capacity boiler, equipped with roller bearings on all engine and tender wheels, one-piece cast steel bed frame, improved counterbalancing, and complete mechanical and pressure lubrication.

The principal advantages of modern coal-burning steam locomotives in comparison with other types of motive power were considered by the Norfolk and Western to be three: low initial cost, high availability and low maintenance cost.

The modern steam locomotives of the Norfolk and Western were essentially of three types:

1. Streamlined passenger locomotive, Class J, with a 4-8-4 wheel arrangement.

2. Single expansion articulated freight and heavy passenger locomotive, Class A, with a 2-6-6-4 wheel arrangement.

3. A compound Mallet heavy freight locomotive, Class Y6, with a 2-8-8-2 wheel arrangement.

Photographs of these locomotives are shown on these and the following pages, together with brief descriptions, including data on the performance, maintenance cost, fuel economy, and utilization of these types of locomotives.

The type 4-8-4 Class J locomotive had a calculated tractive effort of 80,000 pounds, was 109 feet 2-1/4 inches over all in length, and the engine and tender weighed 872,600 pounds. This locomotive was equipped with cast steel bed frame, roller bearings on the engine truck, drivers, trailing truck and tender truck journals, and on the wrist and crank pins and valve gear. It had light weight rods and reciprocating parts, and mechanical lubrication to a total of 220 points. The mechanical lubricators had a capacity sufficient to operate 1,300 miles without replenishment. The roller bearings on the crank and wrist pins had sufficient lubrication capacity to run 500 miles without replenishment. On extended runs these crank and wrist pins could be refilled in station stop time. The drawbar

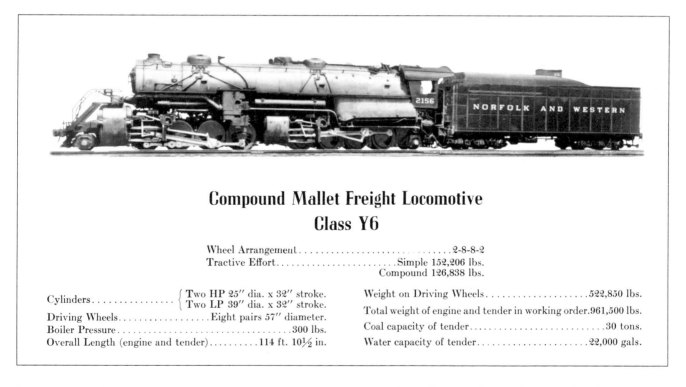

Single Expansion Articulated Freight and Passenger Locomotive
Class A

Wheel Arrangement............................2-6-6-4
Tractive Effort............................114,000 lbs.

Cylinders.....................Four 24″ dia. x 30″ stroke.	Weight on Driving Wheels...................432,350 lbs.
Driving Wheels...................Six pairs 70″ diameter.	Total weight of engine and tender in working order.951,600 lbs.
Boiler Pressure..................................300 lbs.	Coal capacity of tender...........................30 tons.
Overall Length (engine and tender)..........121 ft. 9¼ in.	Water capacity of tender.....................22,000 gals.

Compound Mallet Freight Locomotive
Class Y6

Wheel Arrangement............................2-8-8-2
Tractive Effort......................Simple 152,206 lbs.
Compound 126,838 lbs.

Cylinders............... { Two HP 25″ dia. x 32″ stroke. { Two LP 39″ dia. x 32″ stroke.	Weight on Driving Wheels...................522,850 lbs.
Driving Wheels.................Eight pairs 57″ diameter.	Total weight of engine and tender in working order.961,500 lbs.
Boiler Pressure..................................300 lbs.	Coal capacity of tender...........................30 tons.
Overall Length (engine and tender).........114 ft. 10½ in.	Water capacity of tender.....................22,000 gals.

horsepower of this locomotive was rated well in excess of 5,000.

The Class J locomotives were primarily designed to handle heavy passenger trains over mountain grades, but where grades and curvature permitted, speeds in excess of 100 miles per hour were recorded. These locomotives had an assignment of approximately 15,000 miles per month per locomotive and accumulated an average of 238,000 miles per locomotive before first stopping for classified repairs was necessary.

The type 2-6-6-4 Class A was a single expansion articulated locomotive, 121 feet 9-1/4 inches over all in length, had a calculated tractive effort of 114,000 pounds, and the weight of engine and tender in working order was 951,600 pounds.

73

These locomotives were equipped with cast steel bed frames, roller bearings on the engine trucks, drivers, trailing truck and tender truck journals, and mechanical lubrication to a total of 238 points. The maximum sustained drawbar horsepower, as determined by dynamometer records, was 6,300 at 45 miles per hour. The maximum rate of evaporation recorded was 116,055 pounds of water per hour, or approximately 14,000 gallons. The top sustained combustion rate was 7 tons per hour.

This was a versatile type locomotive used for slow freight service in certain districts, for time freight service in other districts and for heavy passenger train movement over practically all main line districts. In passenger service, this engine delivered sustained speeds of over 70 miles an hour.

The type 2-8-8-2 compound Mallet locomotive, Class Y6, was 114 feet 10-1/2 inches overall in length, had a calculated tractive effort of 126,838 pounds in compound and 152,206 pounds in simple position, and the engine and tender weighed 961,500 pounds in working order.

These locomotives were equipped with cast steel bed frames, roller bearings on the engine trucks, drivers, trailing truck journals, and had mechanical lubrication to a total of 213 points

Above: The three types of advanced steam locomotives used by the Norfolk & Western in the early postwar era, and covered in detail in this chapter, appear together above.

Opposite: The front cover of the Pennsylvania Railroad's centennial booklet.

throughout the engine.

This type locomotive was assigned to both time and slow freight service in mountainous territory. Where operating conditions permitted, they attained top speeds of 45 to 50 miles per hour with tonnage trains.

It is ironic that while these types of steam locomotives were among the last of their breed, they achieved a state of perfection hardly dreamt of as recently as the turn of the century. Compared with the conventional type engine constructed in 1920, these engines required approximately 23% less coal per thousand gross ton miles of traffic handled, and cost 19% to 37% less to maintain per million tractive power pound miles. To express the figures in another way, the conventional type steam engine, built in 1920 cost over 50% more to maintain for the same amount of service delivered than did the steam engines detailed on these pages.

1846 1946

One Hundred Years

OF TRANSPORTATION PROGRESS

—

PENNSYLVANIA RAILROAD

CHAPTER THREE
American Presidents and American Railroads

For more than 100 years, the steam railroads were so completely interwoven into the fabric of American life that no aspect of American commerce or culture escaped their influence. This influence extended as high as the White House itself-- hardly surprising since the presidency is usually not far from the center of things. Along the way, Presidents of the United States supported innumerable laws advancing the cause of the steam railroad. In time, Presidents even learned to use the steam railroads in their personal political campaigns. And, too, presidential funeral trains became the public focus of more than one national tragedy.

Andrew Jackson was the first President of the United States to ride on a steam train. This event took place on June, 1833, on the Baltimore & Ohio between Ellicott's Mills and Baltimore, Maryland-- the same 13 mile run that had recently figured in the celebrated race of the Tom Thumb.

Martin Van Buren--Jackson's vice-president--succeeded him in office and, in 1838, signed the act establishing railway mail service. William Henry Harrison, who followed Van Buren, became the first President for whom a funeral train was used, in April, 1841. Harrison was the oldest president ever elected until Ronald Reagan, and survived barely a month in office.

Zachary Taylor, in his annual message in December, 1849, was the first president to advocate the construction of a transcontinental railroad. Millard Fillmore, who succeeded to the office upon Taylor's death, signed the first railroad land-grant act on September 20, 1850. He also personally opened the first direct rail route from the Hudson River to Lake Erie, on May 14-15, 1851.

James Buchanan was president of the Harrisburg, Portsmouth, Mount Joy & Lancaster Railroad in Pennsylvania, in the 1830's. This railroad later became a part of the main line of the Pennsylvania Railroad. Buchanan, the nation's only bachelor president, served just prior to the outbreak of the Civil War.

Abraham Lincoln, who followed Buchanan, had been an attorney for the Illinois Central and Rock Island railroads in Illinois during the 1850's. His funeral train, following his

assassination on April 14, 1865, was one of the saddest--and most famous--trains in American history as it cut a swath across the North from Washington to New York, then through Chicago to Lincoln's final resting place in Springfield, Illinois.

Lincoln's funeral car had recently been built for his official use and that of his cabinet. On April 21, 1865, the car accompanied by six others pulled out of Washington to commence the final journey. All seven cars and the locomotive were draped in black. On May 3rd, the train at last reached Springfield, Illinois.

Andrew Johnson, in 1866, was the first President to make a tour of the states by rail. This was the original "Swing Around the Circle" during which Johnson tried without success to rally public support for his conciliatory policies toward the defeated South. This was not the first time Johnson had had a bad experience on a train trip. After Tennessee seceded from the Union at the outbreak of the Civil War, Johnson, then a United States Senator, had become one of a handful of Southern politicians to remain in Congress and refuse to secede with their states. On a trip home shortly thereafter, Johnson was nearly hanged by a murderous mob in Lynchburg, Virginia. They only spared his life when someone suggested that the honor of stringing him up should be left to his own constituents. This incident was the origin of the term "lynching."

Ulysses S. Grant, who was elected after Johnson, signed a joint resolution of Congress on April 10, 1869, designating the common terminus of the Union Pacific and Central Pacific railroads, thus facilitating the historic joining of the nation by rails at Promontory Point, Utah.

Rutherford B. Hayes was probably the only President of the United States who received news of his election while riding on a train. Due to political turmoil, the formal declaration of his election had been delayed by the Electoral College. He finally received word on March 2, 1877, while en route to Washington, D.C.

In 1881, James A. Garfield was shot in the Baltimore & Ohio train station, located in the middle of what is now the Mall in Washington, D.C. Mortally wounded, he was eventually taken by train to his summer home on the New Jersey coast where he died. His funeral train became another focal point of grief for the nation.

Chester A. Arthur, who became president upon Garfield's death, participated in the opening of the first railroad to the Pacific Northwest on September 8, 1883. Grover Cleveland, who followed Arthur, signed the original "Act to Regulate Interstate Commerce" on February 4, 1887. He also appointed the first commission.

Benjamin Harrison, on April 29 and

This souvernir card, left, was distributed at the Grand Army of the Republic's (G.A.R.) annual "encampment" in 1908. The card was published by the Lamson Brothers Company of Toledo, Ohio. The firm's founder, Myron Lamson, had been, as an enlisted man, the foreman of the crew that built the car and, later, remodeled it for its funeral duties.

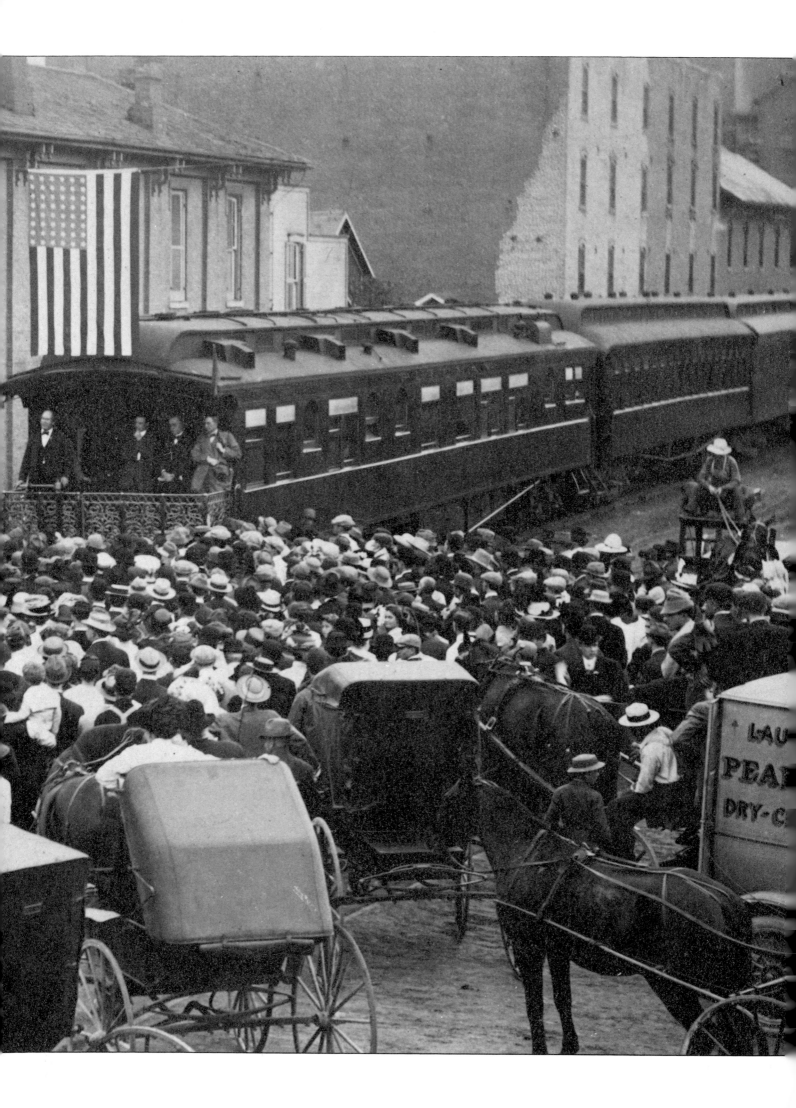

May 2, 1889, made a round-trip by rail to New York from Washington, D.C., for the centennial celebration of George Washington's inauguration. Harrison made the trip to New York in 5-1/2 hours, compared to the 7 days it took Washington to make the same journey. Harrison was also a noted railroad attorney in private life--like Abraham Lincoln before him.

William McKinley traveled more extensively by train than any other previous President, making more than 40 railroad journeys out of Washington between 1897 and 1901. The railroads played a significant part in his election campaigns, as well. His opponent in both 1896 and 1900 was William Jennings Bryan, the first politician to actively take his presidential case to the people. Until that time, it had been thought unseemly for a presidential candidate to actively campaign. The office was supposed to seek the man, not the other way around. This was not good enough for Bryan; he charged around the country like a man possessed, exhorting enthusiastic crowds from the rear platform of his campaign train. Meanwhile, McKinley conducted a more traditional "front porch campaign" from his home in Canton, Ohio. The Republican Party paid to have tens of thousands of voters brought by train to Canton to hear McKinley speak--bringing the mountain to Mohammed, as it were. McKinley won the election but Bryan set the campaign style that all future presidential candidates would have to follow. Going to the people became the only way to get elected in the 20th Century. Only a few years later, William Howard Taft traveled an astonishing 114,559 miles by rail in one Presidential term--the all-time record for presidential rail travel on an annual basis.

The Federal Government, by proclamation

Previous pages: A souvenir postcard of the election of 1896 sent by a Bryan supporter from one of countless speaking stops along the route of the campaign train. The supporter wrote: "This is a picture of the group that heard Bryan speak here about 2 weeks ago. The one with the circle around is me; I had no coat on, and had on a cloth hat as you will see."

of President Woodrow Wilson, took control of and operated the railroads of the country from January 1, 1918 to March 1, 1920, during World War I. Wilson, on September 3, 1919, inaugurated the practice of transacting White House business in an office car on a presidential train. This practice was only abandoned with the advent of practical commercial aviation.

When President Warren Harding died in San Francisco, in 1923, of heart failure, his body was returned to Washington, D.C., in yet another funeral train. Traversing well over three thousand miles, Harding set a record not only for the distance of funeral trains but also for the distance away from the White House at his time of death of an American President.

Presidential use of the rails reached its zenith toward the end of the steam era. Franklin D. Roosevelt's journeys by rail totaled 243,827 miles during his 12 years and one month in office, a total greater than that of any other President. His death in 1945 was the occasion for the last great presidential funeral train.

Harry S. Truman had been a timekeeper on the construction of the Santa Fe Railway around 1901. His "give 'em Hell" campaign across the country by train in 1948--reminiscent of Bryan's original campaign by rail--became one of the most celebrated presidential campaigns in modern American history.

After Truman, presidents increasingly relied on air to press their cases with the people. Although campaign trains figured in some way as late as the Nixon-Humphrey-Wallace contest in 1968, air travel at last became the normal way to campaign for president and travel to and from the White House.

The train carrying the body of President Harding--one of two Presidential funeral trains this century--appears in the photo card on these pages. A hand-written notation on the back states: "Funeral train bearing the body of the late Pres. Harding going slowly eastward Aug. 6, 1923. Photo taken east of Ogden just as the train was about to cross the High Bridge."

CHAPTER FOUR
Some Interesting Technical Information, Facts and Trivia

Getting down to basics, all a steam locomotive really consists of is a steam engine mounted on wheels of a design and width suitable for a particular line of track. Some rather primitive devices have satisfied the criteria over the years--especially in the early years--and, while the mechanism of a 2-8-8-8-2 Mallet Triple Articulated locomotive is numbingly complex by comparison, its governing principles are basically the same.

The idea for a steam engine has been traced at least as far back as 250 B.C. Hero, the Egyptian philosopher, described such devices in a way that leads to the impression they had been around for quite some time even then! True, the steam engines of which he wrote were used for opening temple doors, operating fountains, and the like, rather than for transportation, but the governing principles were much the same.

The first modern use of a steam engine is frequently credited to Edward Somerset, the second Marquis of Worcester. In 1665, he invented a steam engine he called a "water commanding engine" for the purpose of pumping water on the grounds of his castle.

The pumping of water seems to have been of particularly keen interest at this time, for the next landmark in the development of steam was another pumping device--Thomas Savery's "fire engine" of 1698. This engine proved itself capable of pumping thousands of gallons of water per hour and was soon a common feature in British mines, where water seepage had been a frequently lethal problem for centuries. In 1705, Thomas Newcomen invented an improved steam pumping engine that was one of the first to make use of a piston-and-cylinder arrangement.

Thus, by the beginning of the 18th Century, virtually every feature of the practical steam engine as we know it today was devised and in use. All that was lacking was for someone to synthesize all of these developments in one engine capable of taking full advantage of the technology.

James Watt is generally regarded as the father of the modern steam engine. In 1774, he designed and built the steam engine illustrated below. It was loosely based on the Newcomen engine, but was the first to make use of the expansive force of steam. In fact, as Watt realised,

steam expands to more than 1,600 times the space of the water used to make it. Until that point, all steam engines had used steam to facilitate the work being done. Watt, noting the astonishing propensity of steam to expand under pressure, used that property to do the actual work in his machine. He heated water to produce steam, released that steam under pressure into the cylinder chamber where it expanded and pushed the piston. In so doing, he crossed an important threshhold and, in fact, the Watt engine was, with numerous refinements, the one used by all steam locomotives through the era of steam (fig. 1).

Up to this point, however, the steam engine had been used exclusively as a stationary engine, even though Watt, among others, recognized their motive possibilities. The first actual locomotive was built in 1804 by Richard Trevithick, who became the first man to haul carriages on a railroad. This engine, illustrated below, had a cylindrical boiler and a single, vertical piston. There was no condenser of any kind, the steam being exhausted directly into the smokestack.

The Trevithick engine (see the illustration below fig.2) was practical as far as it went, but it was George Stephenson who is generally credited with development of the first modern steam locomotive. His first such engine was built in 1814 and he went on to build many increasingly successful engines until he developed his celebrated

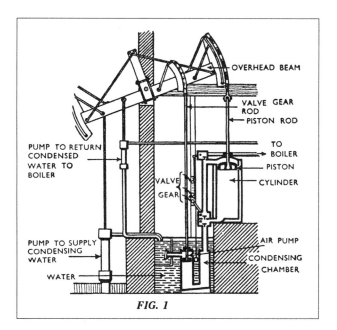

FIG. 1

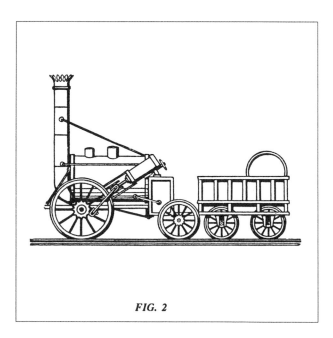

FIG. 2

83

"Rocket" of 1829. The Rocket influenced tremendously locomotive design on both sides of the Atlantic and may be considered the practical common ancestor of all American and British locomotives that were to follow.

How a Locomotive Works

In basic design, the steam locomotive is rather simple and can, for purposes of discussion, be divided into two principal parts. They are the boiler and the chassis.

The boiler, in turn, consists of the firebox in which the wood or coal is burned, a series of tubes through which the gases and steam are carried and a smokestack through which excess gases and steam are exhausted.

The chassis consists of the frame upon which the entire mechanism is mounted, the driving wheels and subsidiary wheels, and the cylinders and pistons through which the power in the steam is turned into a motive force that propels the locomotive.

A diagram of a typical boiler is reproduced below (fig.3). The boiler tubes are located in the lower half of the boiler proper and are the tubes through which the combustion gases are drawn. The super-heater tubes are located in the upper half of the boiler. The super-heater tubes collect at the front of the boiler at the super-heater header, sort of a junction box for both the steam that is due to be super-heated and the steam that has already been super-heated. The steam dome, which is located at the very top of the boiler, feeds into the dry pipe.

The commodity that makes it all work, of course, was the fuel. Originally, the fuel was wood, but coal soon became the standard fuel for steam locomotives on both sides of the Atlantic. The coal is shoveled onto the grates of the firebed where it is burned. The hot gas from the burning coal is then drawn from the firebed through the boiler tubes to the smokebox at the front of the locomotive. In the smoke box, a draft is created by directing the spent steam coming from the driving cylinders up the smokestack.

Meanwhile, the water in the boiler has been heated to the point where steam has been created and is collecting at the top of the boiler in the vicinity of the steam dome. At this point, steam is drawn off into the dry pipe and circulated downward through the super-heater tubes where it is heated some more (super-heated) before being vented into the driving cylinders to do its work of moving the pistons and, with them, the locomotive. Water that is lost is replaced from the tender.

The average road locomotive in service on the railroads of the United States at the peak of the steam era had approximately one mile of boiler tubing. The aggregate length of the boiler tubing in a 4-8-4 type of locomotive was 1.05 miles; in a Mallet type, 1.3 miles.

The water capacity of passenger locomotive tenders of the types commonly in use right after the war, ranged from 4,000 to 25,000 gallons, with the

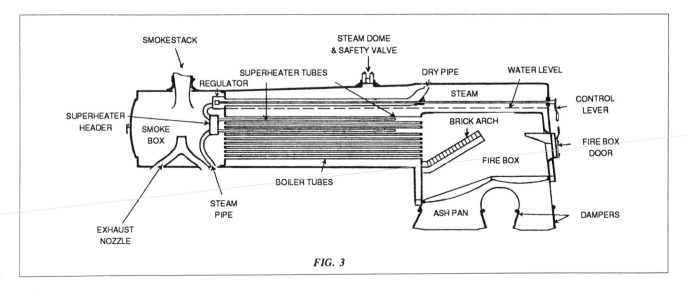

FIG. 3

average between 16,000 and 20,000 gallons. The capacity of tenders employed in freight service ranged from 8,800 to 26,500 gallons, the most common being from 16,000 to 22,000 gallons. The tender capacity of switch engines ranged from 6,000 to 19,000 gallons, with 9,000 to 10,000 gallons capacity the most commonly used.

The fuel--i.e., coal--capacity of coal-fired passenger locomotive tenders ranged from 6 to 46 tons with an average of from 15 to 26 tons. Freight locomotive tenders carried from 12 to 43 tons, 16 to 30 tons being the average. The fuel capacity of switch engine tenders ranged from 8 to 25 tons, the most common being 10 to 12 tons. The fuel capacity of oil-fired steam locomotive tenders, both passenger and freight, ranged from 4,000 to 7,000 gallons of fuel oil.

The tractive force of the average steam locomotive on the Class I railroads of the United States was 39,177 pounds in 1923, and 54,506 pounds in 1948--an increase of 39 per cent during the last twenty-five years of the steam era.

Wheel Arrangements

The different types of locomotives were generally, and most easily, identified by their wheel arrangements. The Whyte System came to be regarded as the standard system of classification for locomotive types and it is that system that has been used in this book.

Classifications by wheel arrangements are shown in the table below. For instance, a Pacific type locomotive has two pairs (4) of small wheels in front, three pairs (6) of drivers, followed by a single pair (2) of small wheels under the cab. Thus, the engine is known as a 4-6-2, or Pacific type. The following table will enable anyone to identify nearly every locomotive operated on the American railroads. Always start at the front of the engine and read back. Note, also, that there are a few classifications that do not have type designations. There are also some types that have more than one designation. The Northern type, for example, was also known as the Dixie, Greebrier, Confederation, Pocono, Niagara or Wyoming type:

Symbol	Front to Back	Type
0-4-0	OO	4-Wheel Switcher
0-6-0	OOO	6-Wheel Switcher
0-6-6-0	OOO OOO	Mallet Articulated
0-8-0	OOOO	8-Wheel Switcher
0-8-8-0	OOOO OOOO	Mallet Articulated
0-10-0	OOOOO	10-Wheel Switcher
2-4-4-2	o OO OO o	Mallet Articulated
2-6-0	o OOO	Mogul
2-6-2	o OOO o	Prairie
2-6-4	o OOO oo	
2-6-6-0	o OOO OOO	Mallet Articulated
2-6-6-2	o OOO OOO o	Mallet Articulated
2-6-6-4	o OOO OOO oo	Mallet Articulated
2-6-6-6	o OOO OOO ooo	Allegheny
2-8-0	o OOOO	Consolidation
2-8-2	o OOOO o	Mikado
2-8-4	o OOOO oo	Berkshire
2-8-8-0	o OOOO OOOO	Mallet Articulated
2-8-8-2	o OOOO OOOO o	Mallet Articulated
2-8-8-4	o OOOO OOOO oo	Yellowstone
2-8-8-8-2	o OOOO OOOO OOOO o	Triple Articulated
2-10-0	o OOOOO	Decapod
2-10-2	o OOOOO o	Santa te
2-10-4	o OOOOO oo	Texas
2-10-10-2	o OOOOO OOOOO o	Mallet Articulated
4-4-0	oo OO	American
4-4-2	oo OO o	Atlantic
4-4-4	oo OO oo	
4-4-4-4	ooOO OOoo	*
4-4-6-4	ooOO OOOoo	*
4-6-0	oo OOO	10-Wheel
4-6-2	oo OOO o	Pacific
4-6-4	oo OOO oo	Hudson
4-6-6	oo OOO ooo	
4-6-4-4	oo OOO OO oo	*
4-6-6-4	oo OOO OOO oo	Challenger
4-8-0	oo OOOO	Mastodon
4-8-2	oo OOOO o	Mountain
4-8-4	oo OOOO oo	Northern
4-8-8-2	oo OOOO OOOO o	Mallet Articulated
4-8-8-4	oo OOOO OOOO oo	Big Boy
4-10-0	oo OOOOO	Mastodon
4-10-2	oo OOOOO o	Southern Pacific
4-12-2	oo OOOOOO o	Union Pacific
6-4-4-6	ooo OO OO ooo	*
6-8-6	ooo OOOO ooo	Steam-Turbine

*4 cylinder non-articulated

85

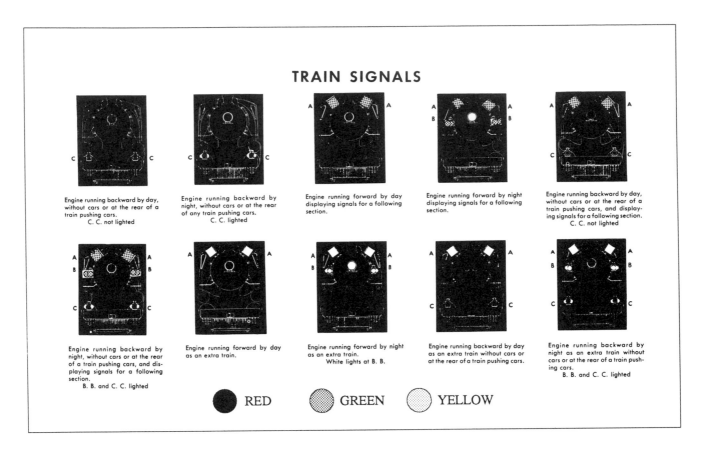

TRAIN SIGNALS

Engine running backward by day, without cars or at the rear of a train pushing cars.
C. C. not lighted

Engine running backward by night, without cars or at the rear of any train pushing cars.
C. C. lighted

Engine running forward by day displaying signals for a following section.

Engine running forward by night displaying signals for a following section.

Engine running backward by day, without cars or at the rear of a train pushing cars, and displaying signals for a following section.
C. C. not lighted

Engine running backward by night, without cars or at the rear of a train pushing cars, and displaying signals for a following section.
B. B. and C. C. lighted

Engine running forward by day as an extra train.

Engine running forward by night as an extra train.
White lights at B. B.

Engine running backward by day as an extra train without cars or at the rear of a train pushing cars.

Engine running backward by night as an extra train without cars or at the rear of a train pushing cars.
B. B. and C. C. lighted

● RED   ◉ GREEN   ○ YELLOW

How Much Coal Does a Steam Locomotive Consume?

The distance depends upon the locomotive, the weather, the train load and other factors, but the average locomotive in passenger or freight service consumes approximately one ton of coal for each 7 miles of travel.

From 1921 to 1947, the amount of coal (or its equivalent) consumed in locomotives on Class I railroads was reduced from 162 pounds to 114 pounds for each 1,000 ton-miles of freight service performed, and from 17.7 pounds to 15.9 pounds for each passenger-car mile of service performed.

Is Regular Tap Water Used?

Railroads found that water which is properly treated chemically greatly increased the efficiency of locomotives and the life of boilers and tubes. Chemical treatment of water prevented erosions or corrosions within the boilers and tubes, reduced the frequency of boiler washings and saved the railroads millions of dollars annually.

How Much Do Steam Locomotives Weigh?

Weights of steam locomotives varied greatly. The weights of freight locomotives purchased during the five-year period 1943-1947 ranged from 135 tons to 597 tons; those of passenger locomotives ranged from 221 to 370 tons; and those of switching locomotives ranged from 106 to 150 tons. These weights included tenders.

By constrast, weights of standard electric locomotives employed in freight service ranged from 91 to 368 tons; those in passenger service ranged from 234 to 463 tons; those of switchers ranged from 76 to 140 tons. Weights of Diesel-electric locomotives also varied widely. The weights of those employed in freight service ranged from 44 to 222 tons; those employed in passenger service ranged from 103 to 297 tons; those employed in switching service ranged from 25 to 250 tons. Many of the heavier freight and passenger engines were combined in three or four connected units, sometimes called sections.

ENGINE WHISTLE SIGNALS

The signals prescribed are illustrated by "o" for short sounds, "—" for longer sounds; and "—•—" for extra long sounds. The sounds of the whistle should be distinct; short sounds should continue for approximately 1½ to 2 seconds, with a stop of one second; long sounds should continue for approximately 2½ to 3 seconds with a stop of one second; extra long sounds should continue for approximately 5 seconds.

SOUND	INDICATION
o	Apply brakes. Stop.
— —	Release brakes. Proceed.
— o o o	Flagman protect rear of train.
— — — —	(Single and double track). Flagman may return from west or south.
— — — — —	(Single and double track). Flagman may return from east or north.
— — —	When running, train parted; to be repeated until answered by signal prescribed by lamp signal E on lower part of right hand page.
o o	Answer to any signal not otherwise provided for.
o o o	When train is standing, back. Answer to lamp signal D on lower part of right hand page.
o o o o	Call for signals.
— o o	(Single track). To call attention of yard engines, extra trains, or trains of the same or inferior class or inferior right, to signals displayed for following section.
	(Double track). To call attention of yard engines or of trains moving in the same direction to signals displayed for following section.
—•— —•— o o	Approaching public crossings at grade, at curves and other obscure places; to be prolonged or repeated until passed.
—•—	Approaching stations, junctions, railroad crossings and tunnels.
o o —	Second engineman on doubleheader assume control of air brakes.
o —	Inspect train line for leak, or for brakes sticking.

Succession of short sounds. Alarm for persons or live stock on the track.

COMMUNICATING SIGNALS

(Between train crew and engine crew given only from train by pulling air signal cord in the following manner.)

Sound	Indication
o o	When standing—start
o o	When running—stop at once
o o o	When standing—back the train
o o o	When running—stop at next passenger station
o o o o	When standing—apply or release air brakes
o o o o	When running—reduce speed
o o o o o	When standing—recall flagman
o o o o o	When running—increase speed
o	Conductor call engineman's attention to meeting point
o o o o o o	When running—increase train heat
—•— o	When running—shut off train heat
—•—	When running—brakes sticking; look back for hand signals

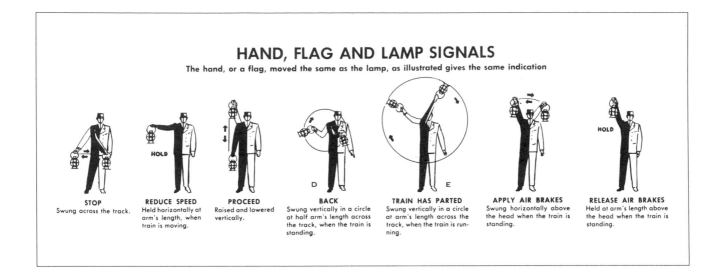

HAND, FLAG AND LAMP SIGNALS

The hand, or a flag, moved the same as the lamp, as illustrated gives the same indication

STOP	REDUCE SPEED	PROCEED	BACK	TRAIN HAS PARTED	APPLY AIR BRAKES	RELEASE AIR BRAKES
Swung across the track.	Held horizontally at arm's length, when train is moving.	Raised and lowered vertically.	Swung vertically in a circle at half arm's length across the track, when the train is standing.	Swung vertically in a circle at arm's length across the track, when the train is running.	Swung horizontally above the head when the train is standing.	Held at arm's length above the head when the train is standing.

According to figures compiled by the Interstate Commerce Commission, as late as 1947, 64 per cent of passenger service was performed by steam, 26 per cent by Diesel-electric, and 6 per cent by electric locomotives and 4 per cent by motorcar-propelled trains. In freight service, 86 per cent was by steam, 12 per cent by Diesel-electric, and 2 per cent by electric locomotives.

What Did a Locomotive Cost?

The average costs of new locomotives installed by the railroads during the five-year period 1943-1947 were as follows:

MINIMUM	MAXIMUM	AVERAGE
Steam, Freight		
$ 88,373	$ 428,598	$ 209,180
Steam, Passenger		
98,742	367,750	177,202
Steam, Switching		
60,610	87,286	77,575
Electric, Freight		
46,960	317,521	272,428
Electric, Passenger		
258,024	464,452	336,892
Diesel-electric, Freight *		
87,448	250,044	137,788
Diesel-electric, Passenger*		
89,744	265,359	174,936
Diesel-electric, Switching*		
14,908	171,521	78,632

*A Diesel-electric locomotive was customarily made up of 1, 2, 3 or even 4 units. The cost figures in this table are for single units, so a 4-unit 6,000 HP Diesel-electric freight locomotive or a 3-unit 6,000 HP Diesel-electric passenger locomotive would have cost upwards of $500,000.

The number of parts and resultant complexity also varied with the type of locomotive and with the specific construction details. A World War II vintage Pacific type steam locomotive had about 25,000 parts, excluding the tender. In a contemorary 2,000 HP Diesel-electric locomotive, it was estimated that there were about 70,000 parts.

What was the Origin of the Caboose?

The caboose was also variously known in the early days as "cabin car," "conductor's car," "brakeman's cab" and "train car." Its exact origin is still something of a mystery.

The cupola, which is a distinctive feature of the modern caboose, seems to have originated as early as 1851, when an "observatory" built on top of a baggage car set out alongside the tracks of the Erie near Suffern, New York, as a temporary telegraph office, suggested the possibility of equipping cars on the road in the same fashion. Independently, the idea occurred to T.B. Watson, a freight conductor of the Chicago & North Western Railroad, who, on a run in Iowa in the summer of 1863, had a way car with a hole in the roof. The resourceful conductor rigged a seat which enabled

AUTOMATIC
BLOCK SEMAPHORE SIGNALS

Three Position
Upper Quadrant Type

Home and Distant
Lower Quadrant Type

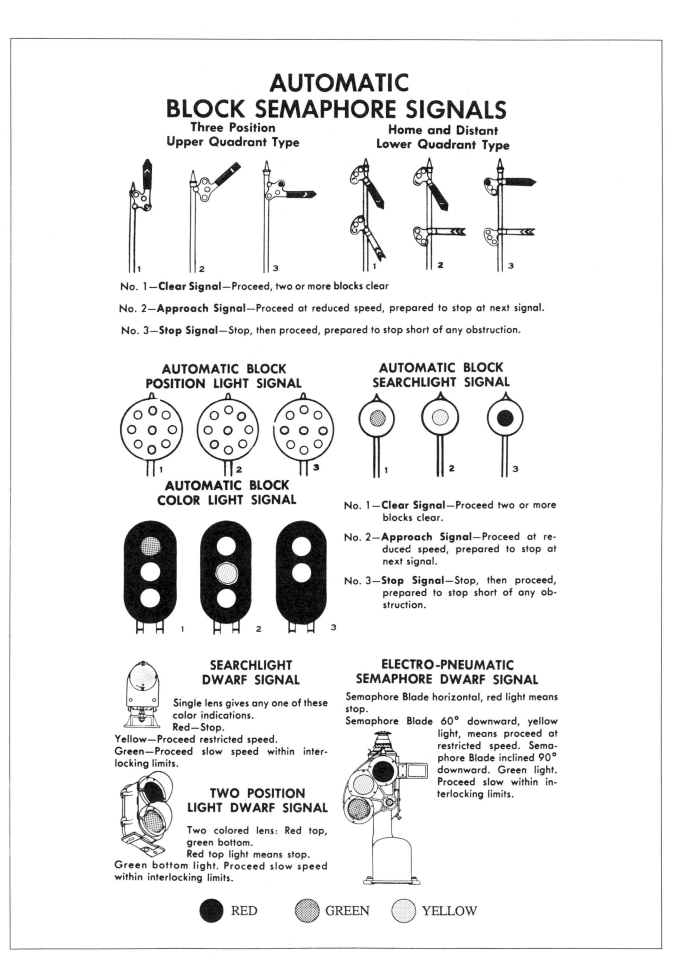

No. 1—**Clear Signal**—Proceed, two or more blocks clear

No. 2—**Approach Signal**—Proceed at reduced speed, prepared to stop at next signal.

No. 3—**Stop Signal**—Stop, then proceed, prepared to stop short of any obstruction.

AUTOMATIC BLOCK
POSITION LIGHT SIGNAL

AUTOMATIC BLOCK
SEARCHLIGHT SIGNAL

AUTOMATIC BLOCK
COLOR LIGHT SIGNAL

No. 1—**Clear Signal**—Proceed two or more blocks clear.

No. 2—**Approach Signal**—Proceed at reduced speed, prepared to stop at next signal.

No. 3—**Stop Signal**—Stop, then proceed, prepared to stop short of any obstruction.

SEARCHLIGHT
DWARF SIGNAL

Single lens gives any one of these color indications.
Red—Stop.
Yellow—Proceed restricted speed.
Green—Proceed slow speed within interlocking limits.

TWO POSITION
LIGHT DWARF SIGNAL

Two colored lens: Red top, green bottom.
Red top light means stop.
Green bottom light. Proceed slow speed within interlocking limits.

ELECTRO-PNEUMATIC
SEMAPHORE DWARF SIGNAL

Semaphore Blade horizontal, red light means stop.
Semaphore Blade 60° downward, yellow light, means proceed at restricted speed. Semaphore Blade inclined 90° downward. Green light. Proceed slow within interlocking limits.

● RED   ◓ GREEN   ○ YELLOW

him to sit with his head and shoulders above the roof. The improved view led him to suggest to the master mechanic at Clinton, Iowa, the building of an elevated glassed-in enclosure on all cabooses.

A new design in cabooses--the bay window caboose--was developed by the Baltimore & Ohio Railroad in 1930. The bay window, which took the place of the cupola, provided trainmen with a side view of the train instead of the conventional roof-top view.

What was the Origin of the Cow Catcher?

The "cow catcher," a strictly American feature, was the invention of Isaac Dripps, a young mechanical engineer employed by the Camden & Amboy Railroad in New Jersey (later to become a part of the Pennsylvania Railroad) in the early 1830's. America was a far more rural place in the early 19th Century than it was to become in later decades and livestock was often permitted to roam freely. So many cows trespassed upon the railroad that Dripps decided to install on the front end of the locomotive a small truck supporting two iron spears. The Dripps device was effective, but lethal (to the cows). To avoid damage suits, he substituted a crosswise bar much like the present-day bumper on an automobile, and from this evolved the present V-shaped cowcatcher.

What was the Origin of Railroad Lighting?

In the early days of railroading, trains ran only in daylight hours and headlights were unknown. As the railroads developed, however, night operations became increasingly necessary and inventive minds went to work to devise ways of illuminating the track ahead. The first crude step was taken under the direction of Horatio Allen, then chief engineer of the South Carolina Railroad. He attached a small flatcar to the front of the locomotive, and covered the floor of the car with a heavy layer of sand on which he kept a bonfire of pine knots. The limitations of this system were obvious. Quite apart from the fire risk, both to the train and to the passing countryside, this method was hardly practical in the rain.

In other instances, large candles protected by glass cases were used with reflectors. Whale oil, a major source of fuel in the mid-19th Century, was extensively used in the 1840s and 1850s. In 1859, kerosene lamps took the place of candles and whale-oil lamps. Then came gas lights, fed from storage tanks, and finally, in 1881, electricity.

Twentieth Century developments included the figure-eight oscillating headlight, first used on the Chicago & North Western in 1936. This was followed in 1944 by an oscillating headlight that would flash either a red or white light, whichever the engineer desired for the purposes of safety. In June, 1946, sealed-beam headlights were first applied by the New York Central Railroad.

Railroad Track Mileage Through the Years

Following is a chart listing American railroad mileage throughout the steam era:

Year	Miles of Road Owned	Miles of Track Operated
1830	23	*
1840	2,818	*
1850	9,021	*
1860	30,626	*
1870	52,922	*
1880	93,296	115,647
1890	163,597	199,876
1900	193,346	258,784
1910	240,439	351,767
1920	252,845	406,580
1930	249,052	429,883
1940	233,670	405,975
1947	225,806	397,355

What was the Railroad Mileage Around the World During the Steam Era?

After World War II, the 783,653 miles of railroad in the world, were distributed as follows:

Continent	Mileage	Per Cent
North and South America	355,536	45.4
Europe	262,172	33.4
Asia	91,872	11.7
Africa	42,074	5.4
Australasia	31,999	4.1
Total	783,653	100.0

What was the Origin of Refrigerator Cars?

The first refrigerator car actually known to have been built in this country began service on the Northern New York Railroad (later part of the Rutland Railroad) on July 1, 1851. On that date, eight tons of butter were transported from Ogdensburg, New York, to Boston in a wooden box car insulated with sawdust. In 1857, thirty insulated box cars were constructed with ice compartments and for the first time fresh meat was shipped from the Chicago Stock Yards to New York and Boston. A southern Illinois fruit grower succeeded in shipping fresh fruit under refrigeration by rail when, in 1866, he sent strawberries from Cobden to Chicago. A refrigerator carload of strawberries shipped from Anna, Illinois, to Chicago in 1872 was the beginning of the successful carload transportation of perishable food.

The first patent for a refrigerator car was issued in November, 1867, and, in 1868, an improved car was designed especially for the handling of meats and fish. With the manufacture of artificial ice in the 1880's, refrigeration became practical throughout the United States. On June 24, 1886, the first special train of fruit to be shipped from California left Sacramento, opening up Eastern markets to shippers.

The phenomenal growth of the market for frozen foods, which required intensive refrigeration in transit, brought about improved refrigerator cars built to standardized dimensions with provisions for easier riding at express train speeds. By the close of the steam era, there were more than 132,000 "Ice Boxes on Wheels"--some of stainless steel or aluminum--being operated on American railroads.

What was the Origin of Circus Trains?

While records indicate that circus travel by rail began as early as December, 1838, with Bacon and Derious' circus, it was not until 1873 that a large circus moved from town to town in trains of its own cars. This was P.T. Barnum's three-ring circus, "Museum, Menagerie, and Hippodrome." More than 60 cars were built to transport the circus, including platform cars, "palace horse cars," and sleeping cars.

What was the Origin of "Railroad" Time?

Beginning in Washington, D.C., at the stroke of 12 o'clock noon on November 18, 1883--and at Noon at designated points in each of the new time zones--about 100 different "times" were abolished in the United States. At that hour, railway clocks and watches throughout the country were set to Standard Time, which, in turn, meant one of four standards of time: Eastern, Central, Mountain, and Pacific.

Standard Time, which soon came into general use in Canada and Mexico, as well, also later influenced the change in time in other Central and South American countries. It was sponsored and put into effect by the General Time Convention of Railway Managers, which later became the Association of American Railroads (which supplied much of the information contained in this chapter).

The purpose of Standard Time was to make life bearable for railroad managers, schedulers and other workers. As the country was increasingly joined by rail and commerce and people increasingly began to flow from town to town, and from state to state, the old system of time was becoming more and more a hindrance to progress. Under the old system, each town or region set its own "sun" time. When the sun reached its apex in Akron, for example, it was Noon. Never mind that Youngstown, 60 miles to the east, recorded a Noon time that was at variance by 3 or 4 minutes. In more sedentary times it had not mattered. By the 1880s it

was beginning to make necessary intercourse between even nearby communities extremely, and needlessly, difficult.

The railroads, upon whom progress depended more than upon any other single activity, demanded rationalization of the confusing time zones. "Railroad" Time was the result. It did the job set for it, but for many years thereafter, old-timers groused about the imposition on them of someone else's time. Progress, as it always does, had exacted a price for its favors.

Previous page: An 0-8-0 switcher not unlike the last one built by the Norfolk and Western Railroad in 1953. Such an engine was the very last steam locomotive built in the United States.

Left and following pages: Sometimes it doesn't pay to get out of bed in the morning. Wrecks, whether due to natural causes or human error, were a constant part of rail life. Along with progress came the occasional disasters; train wrecks killed many over the years. Still, it helps to put such things in perspective. All of the worst train wrecks in the steam era (see Appendix Four for a complete listing), taken together and spanning a period of nearly a century, accounted for fewer than 2,500 deaths. There were half-a-dozen shipwrecks during World War II that, individually, caused more mayhem than that. The worst, the refugee ship "Wilhelm Gustloff," took more than 6,000 people to a watery grave in the early months of 1945. Ironically, the worst recorded train disaster also occurred during that war. On March 2, 1944, 521 people died by asphyxiation in a train en route from Naples to Potenza in Italy. The train entered the narrow, 2-mile long tunnel near Balvano, south of Salerno, at night. Apparently, the train lost traction and the engineer poured on more steam in a futile attempt to make it up the grade. In so doing, investigators surmised, the heavy coal smoke in the tunnel asphyxiated all 521 souls, many as they slept. The engineer was among the dead. Only six persons survived. In contrast, the worst train wreck in American history took 101 lives (at Nashville, Tennessee, in 1918). The runner-up took 97 lives (at New York City, also in 1918).

GERATOR

'CAR.

INVERTED ROOF. BAGGAGE CAR

RECK AT BOONVILLE. N.Y.
JULY. 4. 08.   (NO 9.)

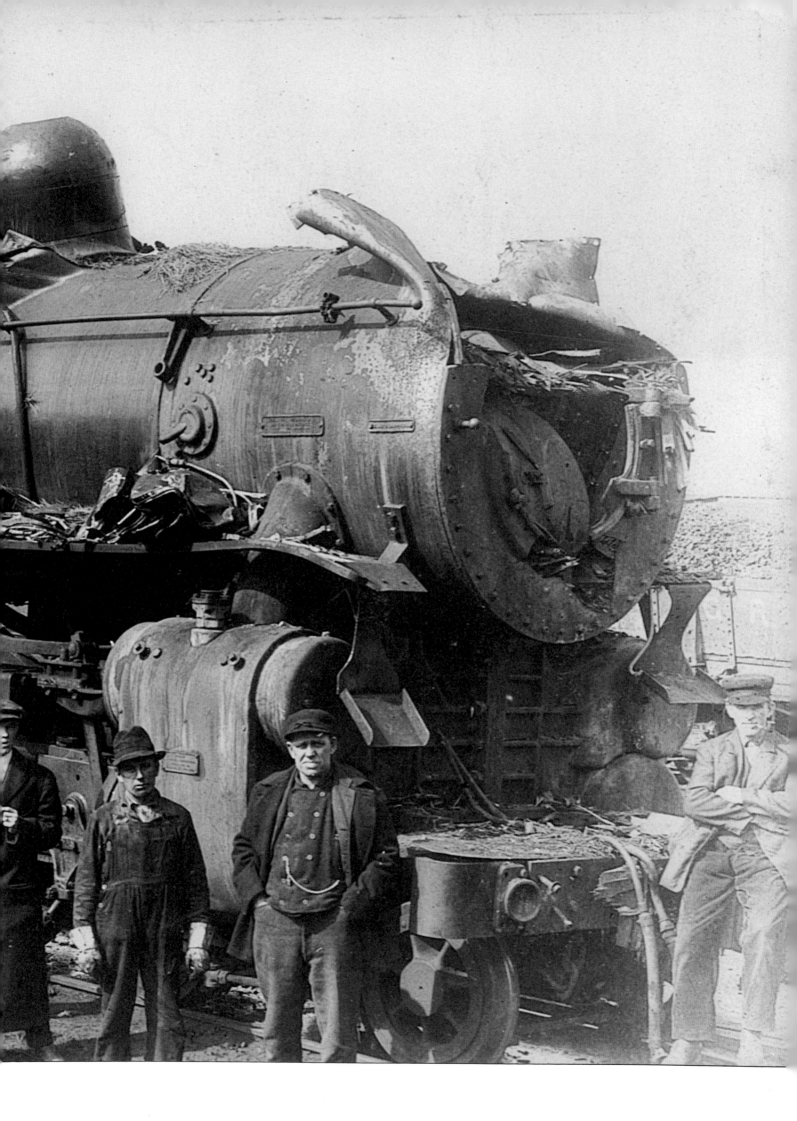

What was the Origin of Train Whistles?

The first locomotive equipped with a whistle is said to have been the "Sandusky," which was built in Paterson, New Jersey. Its first run was made between Paterson, Jersey City and New Brunswick on October 3, 1837.

The Sandusky arrived by water at Sandusky, Ohio, on November 17, 1837, for service on the Mad River & Lake Erie (later a part of the New York Central System). It is said that the gauge (4 feet 10 inches) of the railroad was fixed after arrival of the locomotive.

What was the Origin of Coupling Systems?

In the early days, when cars were small and light and trains were short, a simple coupling known as the "link-and-pin" was used to hold locomotive and cars together in a train. To work this type of coupling, trainmen had to go between the cars to couple them. This, not surprisingly, resulted in many accidents. The method was also slow. As a consequence, many inventors tried to develop automatic couplers and, by 1885, more than 3,100 patents had been issued.

As early as 1869, the Master Car Builders' Association (which later became the Mechanical Division of the Association of American Railroads) began a series of tests extending over many years. An important series of tests beginning at Buffalo, in September, 1885, led, two years later, to the approval by the M.C.B. of a vertical plane automatic coupler invented by Major Eli H. Janney. From then on the Janney type automatic coupler rapidly replaced other types.

Laboratory and field tests were carried on continuously and, in 1916, the type "D" automatic coupler, and, in 1931, the type "E" automatic coupler, were adopted as standard. Following extensive research, a tightlock coupler for passenger train cars was adopted as standard near the conclusion of the steam era, in 1946.

White Mts. N.H., Engine Mt. Washington Railway.

What was the Origin of
the Air Brake?

For more than fifty years following the birth of railroad transportation, speeds were relatively low and trains were generally braked by hand. The first successful application of air to operate brakes was the "straight air brake" patented by George Westinghouse in 1869 which carried all the air for braking purposes in the reservoir of the locomotive.

The next major improvement, in 1872, was the "plain automatic brake," also developed by Westinghouse, which had reservoirs for the storage of compressed air on the individual cars in addition to the main reservoir on the locomotive. With the addition of an ingenious mechanism, called a "triple-valve," a three-way valve interposed between the air line and each reservoir and brake cylinder, the engineer had control of the train at all times through the medium of train pipe pressure and, if the train accidently separated, the car brakes were automatically applied.

By 1884, nearly all passenger cars in the United States were equipped with these brakes. The big problem remaining was a satisfactory brake for freight trains.

In 1886 and 1887, the most complete and exhaustive tests of brakes ever made up to that time were conducted near Burlington, Iowa. Fifty-car freight test trains were operated under all conditions. These tests led to the adoption of an automatic brake with a quick-action triple-valve, an emergency feature which permitted rapid application of the brakes.

A railroad laboratory for air brake tests was

Cogwheel locomotives were specialty types favored by many short run railroads serving mountainous areas. Opposite, an engine from the Mt. Washington Railway in New Hampshire. Below: Colorado's Manitou and Pike's Peak Railway where the average grade was a remarkable 646 feet to the mile.

Following pages: An Illinois Central train loading the car ferry "Pelican" in 1954.

COPR. DETROIT PHOTOGRAPHIC CO.

established at Altoona, Pennsylvania, in 1893; five years later it was moved to Purdue University, Lafayette, Indiana, where facilities for testing brake apparatus were improved and expanded.

Continuous research and tests conducted in extensive laboratories by the railroads and co-operating air brake companies resulted in the development of further improved brake systems permitting quicker service application of the brakes on long trains.

Rack tests at Purdue University, followed by road tests resulted in the adoption in 1933 of the "AB" brake, which made emergency braking available at any time, and permitted fast and positive braking through the train.

Another development, "HSC" electro-pneumatic brakes, first applied on modern high-speed passenger trains in 1933, combined electro-pneumatic, straight air, and automatic air braking. Electric transmission provided simultaneous application and release throughout the train and a device on each axle afforded protection against wheel sliding on wet or icy rails. In the disc brake, developed for use on passenger cars after ten years of research, stationary asbestos-lined shoes gripped both sides of a revolving disc attached to the axle.

Who Was Casey Jones?

The hero of the song "Casey Jones" was a popular locomotive engineer employed in the 1890's on the Mississippi Division of the Illinois Central Railroad. His real name was John Luther Jones, but, to distinguish him from other men named Jones who worked the line, his friends nicknamed him "Casey" in honor of his hometown, Cayce, Kentucky. "Casey" Jones was a strapping young man, black-haired, gray-eyes, 6 feet 4 inches tall, one of four brothers every one of whom was a crack locomotive engineer.

The famous ballad "Casey Jones" originated with Walace Saunders, a negro engine wiper of Jackson, Tennessee, who knew and loved the dashing engineer. Following the news of Casey's heroic death at the throttle of his engine at Vaughan, Mississippi, on April 30, 1900, Wallace,

changing as he worked, put line and line together until they were caught up and passed on by fellow workers to become one of the immortal folksongs of the rails.

Were Individual Steam Locomotives Always Named?

Like ships, many steam locomotives were named. This is certainly true of the early examples, such as the Tom Thumb, the John Bull and the Stourbridge Lion. The practice died out for the most part by the end of the 19th Century.

Locomotive type names were often drawn from the original examples built. For instance, the Central Railroad of New Jersey ordered a 2-6-0 engine in 1866 which it named the Mogul. That name eventually became a generic for all 2-6-0 locomotives.

Patriotism and regional pride entered into it, too. During World War II there was an attempt to rename the 2-8-2 Mikado type the MacArthur and many Southerners referred to the 4-8-4 Northern type as the Dixie!

When was the Last Steam Locomotive Built in America?

The last steam locomotive was a 0-8-0 switcher placed in service by the Norfolk and Western Railroad in 1953. An estimated 133,000 steam engines of all types were built in American shops between 1830 and 1953.

Where Do I Write for Additional Information On Steam Locomotives?

Several important national organizations serve the needs of steam locomotive buffs:

National Railway Historical Society, P.O. Box 2051, Philadelphia, PA 19103.

The Railway & Locomotive Historical Society, P.O. Box 1418, Westford, MA 01886.

The Railroad Enthusiasts, c/o 356 Main St., West Townsend, MA 01474.

ON THE JOB FOR UNCLE SAM

This husky fellow was designed to furnish the motive power for one of the Union Pacific fleet of Limited trains providing comfortable passenger transportation between Chicago and the West Coast. Today, he and many like him are performing an important war-time task. Uncle Sam has called on the railroads, not only to move vast quantities of war materials, but also to transport thousands of men in service. Thus, we are not always able to provide preferred accommodations for civilians who find it necessary to travel. To these patrons, Union Pacific wishes to express its appreciation for their patience and cooperation.

The Progressive

UNION PACIFIC RAILROAD

ROAD OF THE STREAMLINERS AND THE CHALLENGERS

Above: A World War II vintage advertisement from the Union Pacific Railroad. The locomotive is a 4-8-8-4 Big Boy. The Big Boy

weighed over 1.2 million pounds.

Pages 106-107: A 4-6-2 Pacific type from the files of the Erie Railroad.

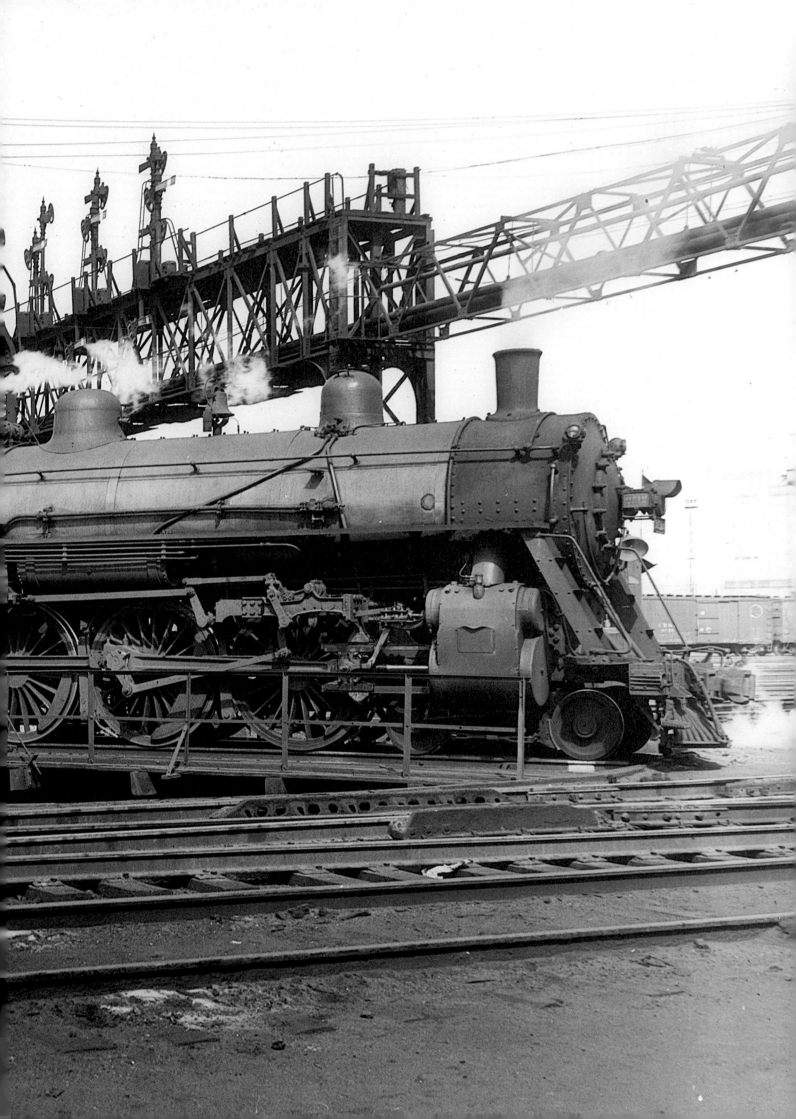

CHAPTER FIVE

Riding the Rails: Train Cars and Interiors

Since from the beginning a primary purpose of the railroads was to carry people, it was not surprising that passenger cars were the subject of continuing, intense attention. The first passenger cars were rather primitive contrivances. Many of the

Dinner anyone? Dining used to be one of the real joys of American rail travel. Needless-to-say, that was before Amtrak discovered fast food. The dining car, above, is Burlington from around 1909. The menu, right, is also Burlington, but from 1934. The special of the day (not on the main menu) was prime ribs for 60¢. Even considering the purchasing power of the Dollar in 1934, that seems a rather good deal.

Previous pages. The Strasburg Rail Road is the oldest short-line steam railroad in the country and still runs a collection of trains for steam buffs daily. On pages 108-109, a 2-10-0 Decapod number 90. On pages 110-111, an E-7 Class Atlantic. Full particulars about these trains appear on page 23 (James R. Moody photos).

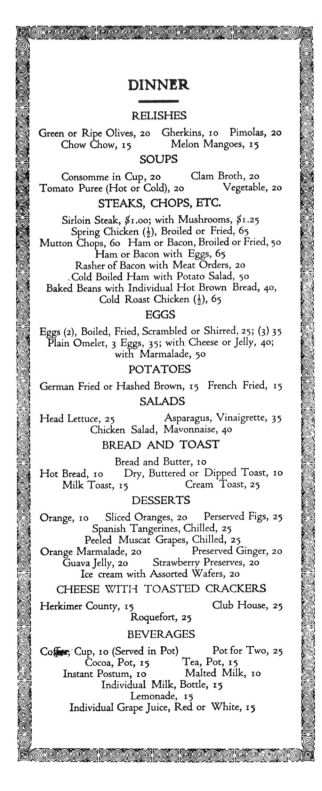

DINNER

RELISHES
Green or Ripe Olives, 20   Gherkins, 10   Pimolas, 20
Chow Chow, 15   Melon Mangoes, 15

SOUPS
Consomme in Cup, 20   Clam Broth, 20
Tomato Puree (Hot or Cold), 20   Vegetable, 20

STEAKS, CHOPS, ETC.
Sirloin Steak, $1.00; with Mushrooms, $1.25
Spring Chicken ($\frac{1}{2}$), Broiled or Fried, 65
Mutton Chops, 60 Ham or Bacon, Broiled or Fried, 50
Ham or Bacon with Eggs, 65
Rasher of Bacon with Meat Orders, 20
Cold Boiled Ham with Potato Salad, 50
Baked Beans with Individual Hot Brown Bread, 40,
Cold Roast Chicken ($\frac{1}{2}$), 65

EGGS
Eggs (2), Boiled, Fried, Scrambled or Shirred, 25; (3) 35
Plain Omelet, 3 Eggs, 35; with Cheese or Jelly, 40;
with Marmalade, 50

POTATOES
German Fried or Hashed Brown, 15 French Fried, 15

SALADS
Head Lettuce, 25   Asparagus, Vinaigrette, 35
Chicken Salad, Mavonnaise, 40

BREAD AND TOAST
Bread and Butter, 10
Hot Bread, 10   Dry, Buttered or Dipped Toast, 10
Milk Toast, 15   Cream Toast, 25

DESSERTS
Orange, 10 Sliced Oranges, 20 Perserved Figs, 25
Spanish Tangerines, Chilled, 25
Peeled Muscat Grapes, Chilled, 25
Orange Marmalade, 20   Preserved Ginger, 20
Guava Jelly, 20   Strawberry Preserves, 20
Ice cream with Assorted Wafers, 20

CHEESE WITH TOASTED CRACKERS
Herkimer County, 15   Club House, 25
Roquefort, 25

BEVERAGES
Coffee, Cup, 10 (Served in Pot)   Pot for Two, 25
Cocoa, Pot, 15   Tea, Pot, 15
Instant Postum, 10   Malted Milk, 10
Individual Milk, Bottle, 15
Lemonade, 15
Individual Grape Juice, Red or White, 15

earliest cars were, literally, stagecoach cars removed from their normal frames and mounted on railroad wheels. Soon, however, cars specifically designed for the demands and desires of railroad passengers began to make their appearance. By the mid-point of the 19th Century, the dining car made its appearance and George Pullman was beginning to revolutionize railroad travel with the cars that were to make his name synonymous with comfortable travel.

The first railway dining cars were operated by the Philadelphia, Wilmington & Baltimore Railroad (now a part of the Pennsylvania) between Philadelphia and Baltimore in 1863. There were two of these cars, remodeled day-coaches, 50 feet in length, each fitted with an eating bar, steam box and "other fixtures usually found in a first-class restaurant," according to an advertisement of the period. The food, however, was prepared at the terminal stations and placed on the cars immediately before the departure of the trains. These primitive "dining cars" remained in operation for about three years. In 1867, George Pullman introduced "hotel cars" (sleeping cars equipped with kitchen and dining facilities) the first three of which were the "President," the "Western World" and the "Kalamazoo." The first Pullman-built car devoted entirely to restaurant purposes was the "Delmonico," operated on the Chicago & Alton Railroad (later part of the Gulf, Mobile & Ohio) in 1868.

By the end of the steam era, a dining car, seating 40 persons, and fully equipped for a total of 500 to 600 services for a round trip, carried approximately 240 tablecloths and tops, 800 napkins, 200 towels, 540 pieces of chinaware, 703 pieces of silverware, 218 pieces of glassware, 240 items of pantry and kitchenware, 20 aprons, 50 waiters'coats, 10 each of cooks' caps and neckerchiefs. It was estimated that railroad dining cars served about 80,000,000 meals in 1947.

Food was not the only problem facing early travelers on America's railroads. Lighting was another critical consideration. In the earliest days, passenger trains ran only in the daytime and did not require artificial lighting. As railroads developed and journeys became longer, night travel came into

LUXURIOUS AIR-CONDITIONED PORTLAND ROSE CLUB CAR
A BLENDED HARMONY OF COLOR AND DECORATION

Above: One of the fast trains on the Union Pacific Line, the "Portland Rose," is depicted here.

vogue, and, as was the custom in stage coaches, passengers brought their own candles. Later, candles were provided by the railroads and protected from drafts by glass shields.

Oil lamps were introduced in 1850 and continued in use for many years. In 1860, gas was first used in car lighting and Pintsch gas was introduced in the early 1880's. Modern electric lighting was first employed in 1885, power being furnished by storage batteries.

The first passenger train in America to be lighted entirely by electricity was operated in 1887. During that year such trains were put into service between Chicago and New York on the Pennsylvania, between Boston and New York on the Boston & Albany and New Haven roads,

113

between Florida and New York on the Atlantic Coast Line, the Florida East Coast, the Richmond, Fredericksburg & Potomac and the Pennsylvania roads, and between Springfield and Northampton, on the Connecticut River Railroad (later part of the Boston & Maine).

From these beginnings, countless improvements continued to be made. Passenger cars of the latter part of the steam era generated their own electricity and were lighted throughout, frequently by fluorescent lights. The first passenger car equipped with fluorescent lighting was operated on the New York Central Railroad in 1938. The first passenger train to be equipped with fluorescent lighting throughout was the streamliner "General Pershing," of the Burlington Railroad, placed in scheduled service between St. Louis and Kansas City on April 30, 1939.

Steam heated passenger cars, doing away with stoves or hot water heaters, were introduced in 1881. Passenger cars were greatly improved in 1903 by the introduction of the vapor system of heating. With this system, live steam from the train line was reduced to vapor at atmospheric pressure

Above: Inside a turn-of-the-century steel sleeper on the Rock Island Line (with the upper berths tucked aout of sight).

and admitted to heating coils inside the car.

In 1857, the Naugatuck Railroad (later a part of the New Haven System) equipped a passenger train with canvas devices which provided covered passageways between cars. This feature remained in use for several years. The modern built-in vestibule embodies a combination of inventions in 1887 by Henry H. Sessions and George Pullman, working independently. They employed a combination of spring buffers, to prevent car swaying and elastic diaphragms on steel frames to form an enclosed passageway between cars. Early in that year, the first complete train to be so equipped was placed in regular service on the Pennsylvania Railroad.

The first sleeping car in the world was operated on the Cumberland Valley Railroad (later a part of the Pennsylvania) between Harrisburg and Chambersburg, Pennsylvania, in the winter of 1836-37. It was a remodeled day-coach, with crudely

114

Above: New bulletins being distributed on the Great Northern's "Oriental Limited." This photograph is probably circa 1905.

built berths or bunks. The car was divided into four compartments, each of which was equipped with three bunks, one above the other, all built along one side of the car. At one end of the car was a wash basin. A wood or coal stove furnished the heat, and candles furnished the illumination.

The next important development occurred in 1858-59, when George Pullman, then a young Chicago contractor, converted two passenger coaches of the Chicago & Alton Railroad (Nos. 9 and 19) into sleeping cars at the railway company's shops in Bloomington, Illinois. The first of these cars--No. 9--made its initial trip from Bloomington to Chicago on the night of September 1, 1859.

Pullman regarded the converted passenger coaches merely as experiments and, at Chicago in 1864, he began building the first real Pullman sleeping car. Up to that time the largest sum ever spent for a railway passenger coach was $5,000. Fully equipped, Pullman's first sleeper, the

"Pioneer," completed and placed in service in 1865, cost a then staggering $20,178.

By the close of the steam era, the Pullman coach became the standard of its type on American railroads. Due to dissimilarities in weight and passenger-carrying capacity of coaches and Pullman sleeping cars, however, there was a wide difference in the cost of providing and handling the two types of equipment. Although the average coach in the early 20th Century was designed to accommodate from two to three times as many passengers as a sleeping car, its average weight was about 25% less. The greater weight of a Pullman sleeping car, as compared with that of a coach, was due to the special equipment and facilities required especially for sleeping car accommodations.

In 1947, the average journey of a Pullman passenger was 643 miles, or about as far from Washington, D.C., to Atlanta, Georgia. In that year, cars operated by the Pullman Company traveled an average distance of 213,507 miles each, equal to more than 67 trips between New York and San Francisco.

There were approximately 45,000 passenger-

train cars on the railroads of the United States at the end of World War II. Of that total, 17,542 were coaches; 14,160 were baggage, express and other non-passenger cars; 6,686 were parlor and sleeping cars; 1,628 were dining cars; 1,693 were United States mail cars; 2,635 were combination coach cars; 354 were observation, club and lounge cars; 150 were troop kitchen cars; and 280 were other passenger-train cars. The Pullman Company owned 5,019 of these cars, and operated 1,052 additional cars under lease.

The first steel Pullman sleeping car was the "Jamestown," exhibited at the Jamestown exposition in 1907. For a round trip of one night in each direction, the usual linen stock for a standard Pullman sleeping car consisted of about 451 pieces, made up of 120 sheets, 120 pillow slips, 200 towels, five porter's coats and six laundry bags. In addition, there were two pillows and two blankets for each berth.

Forty-five laundries handled Pullman linen. If the linen were to come out of the wash at once, it would have totalled 132,340,184 pieces. If these had been hung on clothes lines diagonally across the North American continent, ten lines from Key West, Florida, to Nome, Alaska, would have been

Who said romances only started on shipboard? Obviously, the young man and woman in the scene, above, are destined to be more than seat mates. At least, the elderly lovebirds across the aisle seem to think so. Is that how they met? Titled, "Starting on a Long Journey," this wonderful Alfred James Dewey print dates from about 1910.

Chessie, America's Sleepheart, opposite, was the famous symbol of the C&O Lines.

required to accommodate the wash.

The average cost of new passenger-train cars installed by Class I railroads in the 5-year period 1943-1947 was as follows: Coaches, $79,140 each; combination cars, $77,691; parlor cars, $111,354; dining cars, $104,196; club, lounge and observation cars, $95,110; postal cars, $43,324; baggage, express and other passenger-train cars, $28,325 each. Owing to the scarcity of strategic materials, the construction of standard passenger-train cars was not permitted during World War II.

There were about 26,600 passenger-carrying cars in operation on the Class I railroads of the United States, with Pullman cars included, at the end of the war. Their aggregate seating capacity was

117

about 1,600,000.

The first known instance of the United States mail being transported by rail occurred on the South Carolina Railroad, extending westward from Charleston, South Carolina, in November, 1831. On or about January 1, 1832, the Baltimore & Ohio Railroad began carrying mail between Baltimore and Frederick, Maryland. Shortly after the opening of the latter railroad between Baltimore and Washington in 1835, a car was fitted with a compartment for carrying United States mails between the two cities.

By 1840, railroads had begun to provide special space and facilities for the handling of mail en route, and the American Railroad Journal reported in 1845 that they were furnishing space expressly fitted up for the accommodation of the mail, and for the assortment of letters and papers on the road."

A car equipped for sorting mail en route, as an experimental service designed to speed up the overland mail, was operated on the Hannibal and St. Joseph Railroad (now part of the Burlington) in 1862. On August 28, 1864, the first permanent Railway Post Office car for picking up, sorting and distributing mail en route was placed in operation by the Chicago and North Western on a run from Chicago to Clinton, Iowa.

The first successful streamline passenger car trains were operated in 1934. The Union Pacific aluminum alloy streamliner M-10,000, later christened the "City of Salina," equipped with a distillate-electric locomotive, was delivered to the Union Pacific by the manufacturer at Chicago on February 12, 1934. On January 31, 1935, the train was placed in daily operation between Salina, Kansas, and Kansas City, Missouri.

The stainless steel streamliner "Pioneer Zephyr" of the Chicago, Burlington & Quincy Railroad, the first train of this type to use Diesel power and the first to be placed in scheduled passenger service, was delivered by the manufacturer at Philadelphia on April 18, 1934. On November 11, 1934, the train made its initial run in scheduled passenger train service between Lincoln, Nebraska, and Kansas City, Missouri. It inspired,

among other things, the naming of an automobile: the Lincoln-Zephyr, an early attempt to introduce streamlining to road transportation. By the end of World War II, more than 250 streamline passenger trains were operated in scheduled service on the railroads of the United States.

While there were earlier experiments with "air cooling" of passenger cars, the history of air conditioning as it is known today began with the testing of mechanical air conditioning of sleeping cars by The Pullman Company in 1927-1929, and of coaches by the Baltimore & Ohio in the latter year. In 1930, the B & O put in operation the first mechanically air-conditioned passenger car to remain in continuous service, and, on May 24, 1931, that railroad began operating the world's first completely air-conditioned passenger train. The first completely air-conditioned sleeping car train also began operating on the Baltimore & Ohio, on April 20, 1932.

During the next several years, progress was rapid. By the end of 1940, more than 12,000 air-conditioned passenger cars were in operation. Progress during the World War II was retarded due to the scarcity of strategic materials and manpower, but by the end of the war there were more than 15,000 air-conditioned cars in operation.

Steel-frame cars were introduced in the suburban service of the Illinois Central at Chicago early in 1904. Later in the same year all-steel cars went into service on the first New York City subway. Similar cars for suburban service were built shortly thereafter for the Long Island and the New York Central railroads. The first all-steel passenger coach for use in regular railroad service was introduced on the Pennsylvania in 1906.

The first formal mail car was put into service in 1864. Long before 1944, when the ad, opposite, was run, the railroads had become an integral part of the nation's mail system.

Following pages: When one thinks of long-distance travel by rail in the steam era, one thinks of Pullman cars. The cutaways reproduced here, from a brochure issued in 1929, spectacularly illustrate the development of the Pullman car.

"OLD NO. 9" THE FIRST PULLMAN CAR, 1859 (Above)

THE first Pullman sleeper, built 1859, was a reconstructed day coach, little more than half the later length. Except wheels and axles, it was practically all wood. The roof was flat and so low a tall man was liable to bump his head. The seats were adamantine; two small wood-burning stoves furnished heat. Lighted with candles, it had at each end a small toilet room large enough for one person, with tin wash basin in the open and water from the drinking faucet. There were ten upper and ten lower berths, mattresses and blankets, but no sheets.

THE FIRST REAL PULLMAN SLEEPING CAR, 1865 (Below)

IRST modern sleeper, built 1865, The Pioneer; much longer, higher, wider, than predecessors; railroad bridges and platforms were changed to permit its passage. Here first came the raised upper deck and folding upper berth. Heated from a hot air furnace under the floor, lighted with candles, ventilated through deck windows. Two compartments at each end; eight sections; roomy washroom; black walnut woodwork, much inlay and many mirrors. Fully carpeted, French plush upholstery, good beds, ample bedding. Note the 16 wheels, an experiment tried at this period but later abandoned.

THE STEADY MARCH OF PROGRESS, 1876 (Above)

CENTENIAL year, 1876. The car's length grew from 58 to 70 feet. Oil lamps superseded candles. Air brakes appeared, making for greater speed and safety. A hot water heating system replaced stoves and furnaces. Six-wheel trucks were definitely adopted and overhead tanks with gravity supply system afforded water. Interior finish was in walnut, with carving, inlaying and lacquer work characteristic of the period.

THE CAR VESTIBULE APPEARS, 1887 (Below)

THE car vestibule, marking an historical advance, appeared in 1887, strictly a Pullman invention. At first it merely enclosed a narrow passage between cars, to be widened later to full car width. With twelve sections, drawing room, and smoking room, high backed seats, mahogany finish, much carving and ornamentation, higher windows, rich carpets and upholstery, and increasing elegance throughout, the Pullman was now blossoming into the full glory of the later Victorian period.

COMFORTS AND CONVENIENCES MULTIPLY, 1891 (Above)

THE wide vestibule was now in general use, with anti-telescoping construction. The car was growing longer--it is now 75 feet. Pintsch gas has become the standard illuminant, but electric lights are appearing, the result of long experimentation. The car's exterior is of wood strip sheathing, with ceilings of semi-empire design and the air pressure water supply system has taken the place of hand pump and the gravity system.

THE ALL-STEEL CAR APPEARS, 1907 (Below)

NO other advance in car building made so much for safety as all-steel construction. Following the first experimental steel car, in 1907, the type was adopted in general service in 1910. Length 74 feet; full vestibule; 12 sections, drawing room and smoking room; steel sheathed outside; electric light from axle device; low pressure vapor heat system. Interiors were by this time becoming more quiet and modern, with plain mottled finish, green frieze plush upholstery and green carpets. This was the period of standardization.

REFINEMENTS AND CONVENIENCES, 1920 (Above)

NECESSARILY, the world war period interfered with improvements and advancement, Pullman properties, like other railroad properties being taken over by the Government, but subsequent improvement in travel was rapid. Twice as much light was afforded as before the war. Open plumbing, the dental lavatory, the metal dust deflector at windows, the sliding screen in the car window, the anti-pinch device on doors, the floor light in aisles and the safety ladder made their appearance. Innovations in color schemes, decorations and fittings were prominent factors in postwar development.

THE SINGLE ROOM CAR, 1927 (Below)

THE single room car, for over-night journeys, was a special luxury to a large class
of travelers. It contained 14 rooms, each for a single passenger, with full toilet
facilities, stationary bed across the car, folding washstand with mirror and side lights
above, drop shelf for writing or serving meals, luggage space under bed and in roomy racks, cheval
mirror inside the door and air intake in the door, electric fan, thermos water bottle, and individual
heat control. The bed had box springs and spring mattress. Rooms could be combined into suites.

CHAPTER SIX

Railroads on Parade at the 1939 New York World's Fair

The New York World's Fair of 1939-1940 was probably the most important world's fair in America this century. As the saying goes, almost anybody who was anybody was there, including the railroads. The Pennsylvania Railroad even ran a special train from Penn Station in midtown Manhattan out to the Flushing Meadows site--"10 minutes for 10 cents," they advertised it.

Twenty-seven eastern railroads sponsored an ambitious World's Fair Railroad Exhibit housed in a building that encompassed 150,000 square feet of floor space and cost $1,000,000. The entire

Billed as "The Locomotive of Tomorrow," the experimental Pennsylvania Railroad steam engine, below, was a hit at the Railroads on Parade. This 6-4-4-6 type, also known as the Pennsylvania Class S-1, weighed 1,060,010 pounds.

Railroad Exhibit was supposed to have cost 3-5 million depression-era dollars. Individual exhibits included the historical "Railroads on Parade," and the contemporary "Railroads at Work" and "Railroads in Building." The Railroads on Parade exhibit was the one of prime interest to steam buffs.

Railroads on Parade was more than an exhibit of historic trains; it was an elaborate and extremely ambitious pagent show telling the story of the railroads in America. A flyer handed out at the fair boasted of "4 SHOWS DAILY, 4000 SEATS, 25¢...THE GREATEST SHOW AT THE

THE LOCOMOTIVE OF TOMORROW

AMERICAN RAILROADS

GREATEST OF ALL FAIRS ... 5 Thrilling Acts of Drama, Dancing, Music Comedy! ... Cast of 250 Men and Women ... 50 horses ... 20 Old-time and Modern Locomotives on the World's Largest Stage!" Edward Hungerford staged the spectacle, while no less a figure than Kurt Weill ("Three Penny Opera") was lured into composing the music.

The stage was large enough to hold two giant steam locomotives in the show's grand finale (one of them being the Pennsylvania Class S-1 shown on the previous page) and covered 5.5 acres of space, including not only over a mile of trackage, but a water channel for the demonstration of early watercraft replicas!

The show, itself, began at the New York waterfront circa 1829 with the opening of the Erie Canal, then shifted to Quincy, Massachusetts, for a glimpse of the Granite Railway (America's first), then on to Honesdale, Pennsylvania, for the first running of the Stourbridge Lion. The Best Friend of Charleston and the DeWitt Clinton followed close on the heels of that, and so it went. The race of the Tom Thumb was re-enacted, President-elect Lincoln departed by train for Washington, the golden spike was driven at Promontory Point--there was scarcely a highlight of American railroad history that was not recreated four times daily for the Railroads on Parade show. All that was missing was Cecil B. DeMille and a camera crew!

Right: The Pennsylvania Railroad promoted the fair in brochures and, opposite, in magazine ads.

Two narrow-gauge locomotives from the exhibit appear on the following pages. A train from the Colorado & Southern Railway appears at the bottom. The locomotive is a 2-6-0 type. The odd little 0-4-0, inset, with a 2 ft. gauge, was used on the Northern Pacific Railway.

BARGAIN FARES to the

New York WORLD'S FAIR 1939

APRIL 30 to OCTOBER 31 Incl.

Pennsylvania Railroad

131

Santa Fe

As late as the 1940's, the most romantic call in America still was "Booo-ard!" To many people it still meant adventure and new horizons. And, when one thought of adventure and new horizons, one's thoughts easily turned to the American West. The mind conjured up pictures of the wind whipping waves across prairie grass and grain, of white clouds drifting across blue sky, of snowpeaks and tawny deserts, echoing canyons and lush, timbered valleys. As a creator of romantic images, the American West has had few equals in all the world.

This great American Western empire, from the Missouri and Mississippi to the South Pacific Coast, from the Arkansas River to the Mexican border, was built by railroads--and the greatest builder of all of these was the Santa Fe.

The Santa Fe's builders were not inspired idealists, nor did they build the system to carry the torch of civilization into the West. They did it to make money. Some did, some didn't, but, they all gambled their time, their money and their brains in an era when it wasn't even certain the Union would survive. They went through years of heartache and grim disappointment. Unlike their railroad bretheren in the more civilized East, the engineers and surveyors of the Sante Fe lived hard, tough,

Great Rail Lines of the Steam Era

On these and the following pages are brief histories of seven of the most important railroads of the steam era. These seven lines, between them, did nearly $1 billion in business in 1910. And that, to paraphrase a famous political aphorism, was when $1 billion was real money.

dangerous lives in wild country. Construction crews took their chances with Indian raiders, bad water and the rabble that followed the track. Train crews, operators, station agents lived and worked in peril, not only from lawless men, but from cloudbursts, blizzards and buffalo herds.

The Santa Fe started as a little prairie project in a Kansas frontier town. It was founded by Cyrus K. Holliday, who, in 1859, imposed upon the Kansas territorial legislature to grant a charter to the "Atcheson and Topeka Railroad Company." The new company was incoporated for a million-and-a-half dollars.

The Civil War and economic depression intervened to cause innumerable delays in the beginning of the new line, but, finally in November, 1868, the first shovel full of dirt was turned and the Atcheson and Topeka Railroad was launched as a reality. The ambitious goal was to reach as far west as Sante Fe, New Mexico.

Regularly scheduled service was soon attained--in June, 1869--when the line reached Carbondale, Kansas, a distance of 17 miles. By the end of 1872, the line had been built across Kansas--which had become a state in 1861--westward to Colorado. There existed at that point a main line of 469 miles and a branch line--28 miles long--from Newton to Wichita.

The Rockies were conquered in 1878 when a Sante Fe train reached Raton Pass, 8,000 feet above sea level. After reaching Raton Pass, work was continued on into New Mexico. In February, 1880, the line reached Sante Fe, New Mexico--853 miles from Missouri.

Having achieved their original goal, the directors of the Sante Fe set about achieving an even more ambitious one: reaching the Pacific. By 1885, that goal, too, was reality as the Sante Fe reached

San Diego, California. At the same time, the line gained track rights into Los Angeles--a fact which meant very little in 1885 when Los Angeles was barely a village, but was destined to attain vast importance for the line in future years.

During the 1880s, the Sante Fe built or acquired many lines in Texas and gained access to Amarillo, Fort Worth, Dallas, Houston and Galveston. Regular steamship connections between Galveston and major Eastern ports, such as New York, meant that the Sante Fe now had connections from the Southwest through to the major commercial and population centers of the Eastern United States.

That achieved, the Sante Fe set about to establish connections to the main commercial center of the Midwest: Chicago. This was done by 1887.

The original line was toppled by the financial panic of 1893 and subsequently reorganized as the Atcheson, Topeka and Sante Fe Railroad Company. The new firm continued the policy of aggressive expansion that had characterized its predecessor, with San Francisco being reached by 1900. By the close of the steam era, the Sante Fe could lay claim to more than 13,500 miles of track, stretching from Chicago westward to the Pacific and southward to Mexico and the Gulf.

Indeed, in the 20th Century, the Sante Fe was the way to travel to California. It was national news when the line inaugurated daily service on the Super Chief and El Capitan between Chicago and Los Angeles.

The Super Chief, an all-Pullman luxury train, and the El Capitan, an all streamlined chair-car train, first run in 1936 and 1938, respectively, had a running time between Chicago and Los Angeles of just under 40 hours. (This was 5 hours better than Death Valley Scotty's record-breaking run in 1905!) Both were, alas, diesel-powered by 1948.

Below: The historic Sante Fe Trail.

Through the years of the steam era, the story of the Baltimore & Ohio Railroad paralleled with remarkable closeness the story of the United States. Indeed, John Carroll, one of the signers of the Declaraction of Independence, spoke at innauguration of the line's first service. So, by extension, the Baltimore & Ohio traced its history back to the very founding of the nation itself. With the nation, the Baltimore & Ohio constantly expanded its area, until, by the conclusion of the steam era, there were 11,000 miles of B&O track serving thirteen states and the District of Columbia.

The first American-built locomotive operated on a railroad in America was the "Tom Thumb," given a trial run at Baltimore in September of 1830. Before that, the Tom Thumb had been the loser of a famous race with a horse-drawn railroad car run for a distance of 13 miles between Baltimore and Ellicott City, Maryland. The "York," built by Phineas Davis, in York, Pennsylvania, entered service at Baltimore in 1831.

The Baltimore & Ohio was the first railroad to serve as a public conveyor of passengers and freight, in January, 1830. The road was opened for regular freight and passenger traffic between Baltimore and Ellicott's Mills in May, 1830. Despite the experiments with the steam engines, horses were originally used to pull the cars.

Toward the end of the steam era, the Baltimore & Ohio was the pioneer in the

Previous pages: The "Thatcher Perkins" an 1863 4-6-0 Ten-Wheel type locomotive.
Below: The Capitol Limited.

development of air-conditionting, as well. The first mechanical air-conditioned passenger car (the Martha Washington diner) was placed in regular service by the B&O in 1930. On May 24, 1931, the B&O's Columbian, the first train to be completely equipped with air-conditioned cars, was put in service between New York and Washington. The Baltimore & Ohio was the first Eastern railroad to introduce Stewardess-Nurse service in the late 1930s. And, no story of the B&O would be complete without a mention of its uniquely scenic and historic routes.

Passengers were entranced by the sights they saw from B&O windows--beautiful farmlands rugged mountains and sparkling rivers. Names such as Harper's Ferry brought back memories of forgotten days as the trains wound their way through country where the tread of British regiments once sounded, as well as the whoops of painted warriors. The B&O not only was the most historic of American railroads, but traversed some of the most historic territory in America.

By the late-1940s, the B&O was known more as the "Route of the Diesel-Electric Streamliners" than for its steam locomotives and most of its principal trains were then powered by diesels. The B&O had, on August 22, 1935, placed in service the first diesel-electric locomotive ever to haul passengers on a long distance run.

Below: The National Limited.

Following pages: A 4-6-2 Pacific type locomotive, B&O #175, built by Baldwin Locomotive Works in 1916.

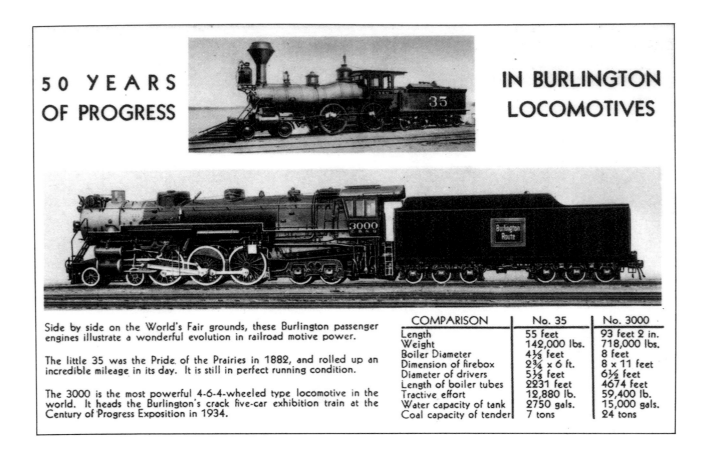

50 YEARS OF PROGRESS ⋅ IN BURLINGTON LOCOMOTIVES

Side by side on the World's Fair grounds, these Burlington passenger engines illustrate a wonderful evolution in railroad motive power.

The little 35 was the Pride of the Prairies in 1882, and rolled up an incredible mileage in its day. It is still in perfect running condition.

The 3000 is the most powerful 4-6-4-wheeled type locomotive in the world. It heads the Burlington's crack five-car exhibition train at the Century of Progress Exposition in 1934.

COMPARISON	No. 35	No. 3000
Length	55 feet	93 feet 2 in.
Weight	142,000 lbs.	718,000 lbs.
Boiler Diameter	4⅓ feet	8 feet
Dimension of firebox	2¾ x 6 ft.	8 x 11 feet
Diameter of drivers	5⅓ feet	6½ feet
Length of boiler tubes	2231 feet	4674 feet
Tractive effort	12,880 lb.	59,400 lb.
Water capacity of tank	2750 gals.	15,000 gals.
Coal capacity of tender	7 tons	24 tons

The Burlington Lines system, which would ulitmately comprise almost 11,000 miles of road in 14 states, had its origin in the tiny Aurora Branch Railroad. A group of citizens in Aurora, Illinois, obtained a charter on February 12, 1849, to build a 12-mile railroad from Aurora to Turner Junction, Illinois, in order to connect with the Galena and Chicago Union Railroad for entry into Chicago.

In 1852, the Aurora Branch Railroad's name was changed to the Chicago and Aurora, and the line was extended westward to Mendota the following year. As the "Central Military Tract Railroad," the line was built to Galesburg in 1854, and, by 1855, the road had crossed Illinois to the edge of the Mississippi River (opposite Burlington, Iowa) with a total mileage of 177. During that year, the Chicago and Aurora, Central Military Tract, and

Peoria and Oquawka railroads were joined, forming the Chicago, Burlington and Quincy Railroad. The new title exactly described the location of the property when, early the following year, a branch from Galesburg to Quincy was completed.

With the C.B.&Q. headed for the Mississippi just across from Burlington, Iowa, in 1854, citizens of that town, with the cooperation of the C.B.&Q., started building the Burlington and Missouri River Railroad to the West. Save for interruption by the Civil War, they kept going until the Missouri River was reached at East Plattsmouth in 1870.

In 1846, the Hannibal & St. Joseph Railroad was chartered and, by 1859, had completed a line across Missouri from Hannibal to St. Joseph. Following the close of the Civil War,

the Hannibal & St. Joseph continued to improve its property. On November 9, 1868, the road obtained a direct physical link with the C.B.&Q. when a bridge was completed over the Mississippi River, and, in 1869, the company opened the first bridge to span the Missouri River and establish through service into Kansas City. In 1883, the St. Joe Line was purchased by the C.B.&Q.

The Hannibal & St. Joseph had the distinction of inaugurating the first United States Railway Post Office. Wm. A. Davis, assistant to the postmaster at St. Joseph, reasoned that if the mail could be sorted on the train itself it could be transferred to the Pony Express immediately upon arrival, thus permitting an earlier start on the long overland race against time en route to California. Two mail cars were built in the Hannibal & St. Joseph shops at Hannibal, Missouri, and sorting the mail in transit began on July 28, 1862.

Meanwhile, the Burlington had continued its expansion westward across Nebraska and Colorado, reaching Denver in 1882. Further large-scale railroad building eventually gave the Burlington a main line from Chicago to St. Paul-Minneapolis, another main line from Kansas City through St. Joseph and Lincoln to Billings, Montana, another line of railroad from Denver to Billings through Central Wyoming, and a major extension of its Illinois lines to the coal fields of Southern Illinois. During this same period of construction and in the years that followed the Burlington either built or acquired scores of branch lines tributary to its main lines, forming rail networks over the rich agricultural regions of northern Illinois, southern Iowa, northern Missouri, and southeastern Nebraska.

Acquisition of the Colorado and Southern lines from Denver to Galveston by Burlington in 1908, and its connections at Billings with the Great Northern and Northern Pacific, provided a tidewater to tidewater line from the Gulf Atlantic to the Puget Sound Pacific--the only diagonal, transcontinental, through route in America.

Regrettably, from the point of view of steam buffs, the Burlington was also in the forefront of diesel locomotive development. A Burlington press release in the 1940s bragged about the "hundreds of modern Burlington...Diesel locomotives [that] have replaced the "tea kettle" engine of Lincoln's day."

The Burlington was the first to introduce the diesel streamlined train in regular passenger service. This forerunner of today's modern streamlined trains ran 1,015 miles non-stop between Chicago and Denver in 1934 at the amazing average speed of 77.6 mph--the original Burlington Zephyr.

The Burlington Zephyr not only foretold the end of the line for "tea kettle" steam engines in the Burlington fleet, it also inspired an automobile of the day: the Lincoln-Zephyr. Edsel Ford, head of Lincoln and son of Henry Ford I, was so deeply impressed with the Burlington Zephyr that he named his new, smaller, and radically streamlined Lincoln after it. The two were even pictured together in some of the early Lincoln-Zephyr magazine ads, although it is not recorded if the Burlington ever returned the favor.

In July, 1945, the Burlington introduced the first Vista Dome car, and in 1947 inaugurated the world's first Vista Dome.

Following pages: A 4-6-4 Hudson type locomotive from the Boston and Maine Railroad. The Hudson type was so called because it was first used by the New York Central and Hudson River Railroad along its Hudson River line. It quickly became popular as a freight hauler with many lines throughout America.

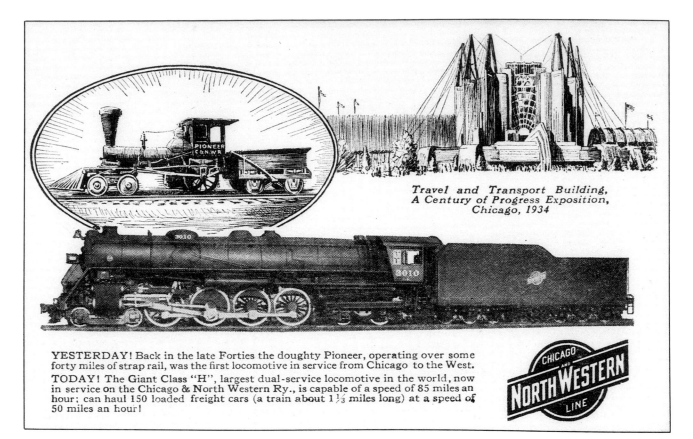

*Travel and Transport Building,
A Century of Progress Exposition,
Chicago, 1934*

YESTERDAY! Back in the late Forties the doughty Pioneer, operating over some forty miles of strap rail, was the first locomotive in service from Chicago to the West.
TODAY! The Giant Class "H", largest dual-service locomotive in the world, now in service on the Chicago & North Western Ry., is capable of a speed of 85 miles an hour; can haul 150 loaded freight cars (a train about 1½ miles long) at a speed of 50 miles an hour!

Chicago, America's second largest city, destined to become the world's most important railroad center, had both its first railroad and its first railroad station in 1848 when the Galena and Chicago Union Railroad began operations. This railroad was the forerunner of the Chicago and North Western. On October 25th in that year, a second hand locomotive--appropriately called the "Pioneer"--which had been purchased in the East and shipped to Chicago on the brig *Buffalo*, was fired up and sent out on iron-capped wooden tracks on a run of 5 miles westward and return.

The Galena and Chicago Union Railroad had been chartered by the Illinois legislature in 1836 but remained on paper for 12 years. Spearheaded by Wm. B. Ogden, Chicago's first mayor, as its president, construction from Chicago toward the West begun in 1848.

The souvenir card, above, was distributed at the Century of Progress Expositon in Chicago in 1934, one of the greatest world's fairs in American history, matched this century only by the 1939 New York World's Fair. Railroad trasnportation was, not surprisingly, an important part of any Chicago fair and the Chicago and North Western Railway System was proudly represented.

Already from the East, three railway lines were building toward Chicago. Farsighted men envisioned the village of Chicago at the foot of Lake Michigan as a potential rail center. Cincinnati, one of the key transportation hubs of the Ohio River, at this time was the most important western center, its prestige and growth having been enhanced by its rail line connection with the Great Lakes at Sandusky, opened in 1848. Cincinnati's population

was 115,000, Chicago's only 30,000, but Chicago loomed large as the gateway to the West, the great unknown West beyond the Mississippi.

The hope of Chicago rested with the invention of the steam locomotive. Chicagoans knew that railroad mileage had expanded in the East from 2,800 miles in 1840 to nearly three times that mileage. As a demonstration of their faith in the new form of transportation embodied in the iron horse, they eagerly contributed their 5 miles to the total of 1,400 miles which had been built in the whole of the United States in 1848.

Within a few weeks after its maiden run, the "Pioneer" brought the first sacks of grain and the first hogs and cattle by rail into Chicago, marking the year that Chicago began to change from a village of retail merchants to a major produce trading center.

Progress for the new rail system was remarkable. By 1864, the Galena and Chicago Union had become the Chicago and North Western Line and had expanded from 10 to 800 miles. Chicago to Milwaukee service had been opened in 1855 and its tracks now extended from Chicago as far west as the Mississippi and were reaching north and northwest into Wisconsin and Minnesota. Another three years of construction, consolidations and acquisitions and the Chicago and North Western, enhanced by feeder lines, also reached across Iowa to Council Bluffs on the Missouri.

Opposite Council Bluffs on the Nebraska side of the river, was Omaha. Ground had been broken there on December 3, 1863, for the construction of the Union Pacific Railroad. The provision for quick and dependable transportation between the East and the Pacific was soon realized. The North Western assisted in this building by hauling great quantities of materials to Council Bluffs for delivery to the Union Pacific. Some of these were hauled by the Pioneer locomotive which had introduced railroading to the West several years earlier. The Central Pacific (now the Southern Pacific) was building eastward from Sacramento to meet the Union Pacific. On May 10, 1869, the two roads met at Promontory, Utah, in one of the watershed events of American history. Five months later, passenger and freight trains were in regular service to the Pacific Coast.

Ever since the joining of the nation at Promontory Point, the North Western, Union Pacific and Southern Pacific cooperated in operating through trains over what came to be known as the Overland Route.

That was the beginning of the pioneer road of Chicago and the West, but pioneering was part and parcel of North Western's development during the steam era, evident in its record of efforts and accomplishments.

By 1926 North Western's expansion had about run its course. It was a vast system of more than 9,000 miles of road, serving nine states direct, its through trains over connecting lines reaching from Chicago to the west coast cities of Portland, San Francisco and Los Angeles.

That same year, 1926, North Western pioneered the use of a diesel-electric locomotive in Chicago, the first used west of New York City. In 1936, in conjunction with the Union Pacific, dieselized streamliners were put in service to the west coast, marking the beginning of the end of the steam era on the North Western system.

In 1935, the North Western introduced a mile-a-minute long distance train in the steam-powered, oil-burning "400"--so named because it covered the 400 miles between Chicago and the Twin Cities of St. Paul-Minneapolis in 400 minutes. This was destined to be the last significant steam development on the North Western system.

On the ninth of August in 1831 a tiny, four-wheeled wood-burning locomotive pulled the first steam-drawn passenger train in the State of New York. With the opening of its throttle the now famous DeWitt Clinton locomotive began more than a century of building on the vast New York Central System. From this single train of the Mohawk & Hudson Rail Road, with its 17 miles of track between Albany and Schenectady, the system grew by the end of the steam era into an 11,000-mile network with some 4,000 locomotives, more than 5,000 passenger cars, 172,000 freight cars and 135,000 employees.

The development of the New York Central went hand in hand with the progress of America. Westward from the Atlantic seaboard went pioneering railroaders contructing lines that bore the names of communities and local areas thcy served. These in turn, through consolidations and reorganizations, became the important railroads in America. The New York Central System was built up this same way through consolidations of the Michigan Central, the Big Four Railroad, the Boston & Albany, the West Shore Railroad, the Pittsburgh & Lake Erie Railroad and others. Through its predecessor roads the New York Central became the first railroad to enter Chicago from the East.

By the apex of the steam era, the New York Central had more multiple track than any other railroad in the world. Noted for its smooth Water Level Route, the New York Central followed gentle river valleys and the shores of the Great Lakes between East and West. Its fleet of passenger trains bore such famous names as the 20th Century Limited, the Commodore Vanderbilt, the Pacemaker, the Southwestern Limited, the James Whitcomb Riley, the New England States, the Mercury, the Detroiter, the Empire State Express and dozens of others.

Within the eleven states and two Canadian provinces served directly by the New York Central lay North America's richest markets, the largest cities and seaports, greatest industrial centers and fertile farm lands, to say nothing of America's historic shrines and favorite holiday resorts, and Central's through car services spanned the nation from the Atlantic to the Pacific, from the Great Lakes to the Gulf states.

Trains traveled for miles along the very edge of such story-book rivers as the majestic Hudson and the historic Mohawk. They passed through Adirondack and Berkshire valleys en route to Montreal and Boston. They skirted the shores of the Great Lakes to Detroit, Toledo, Cleveland and Buffalo and passed within an easy, free side trip to Niagara Falls.

Continuing the pioneering started by the diminutive DeWitt Clinton, New York Central developed many outstanding types of equipment. The famous locomotive 999 achieved 112.5 m.p.h. with the Empire State Express in 1893. It held the world's speed record for many years. The high speed "Hudson" locomotive for passenger service was long the steam rail fan's favorite.

After the war, the New York Central embarked on a $290,000,000 post-war improvement program. Unfortunately for steam buffs, a major part of this program involved the purchase of a fleet of diesel locomotives. With it, the steam era was unfortunately nearing an end in the East.

Previous pages: A late 19th Century 0-8-0 Camelback type locomotive. Following pages: A late 19th Century 2-8-0 Consolidation type locomotive.

Opposite: The great palace of New York Central, the monumental Grand Central Station in New York City.

Grand Central Terminal, New York City.

MAIN CONCOURSE, GRAND CENTRAL TERMINAL,
NEW YORK CITY.

Above: An impressive Pennsylvania 2-10-4 Texas type locomotive.

The story of the Pennsylvania Railroad begins with Colonel John Stevens, America's earliest railroad pioneer. To Stevens on February 6, 1815, was granted the first charter for a railroad in America. The route lay between New Brunswick and Trenton, where the Pennsylvania's New York Division would later be located.

Stevens was considerably ahead of his time in forseeing the emergence of practical rail service. State legislatures all across the eastern United States were being beseiged with plans for the establishment of canal transportation systems. In fact, when the Erie Canal across New York was opened in 1825, Philadelphians demanded a canal route westward to the Ohio River. Although a second charter was granted to Stevens in 1823, actual construction on neither was accomplished.

After 1825, the Pennsylvania legislature granted charters to a few railroads but, being impatient with their progress, decided upon state enterprises to build up the state's transportation

arteries. Despite some services performed by the State Works, they were far from satisfactory and on April 13, 1846, an act incorporating the Pennsylvania Railroad was passed.

The Pennsylvania was originally organized to construct a rail line from Harrisburg to Pittsburgh. Travel between these points was then by canal from Columbia to join the river to the west at Middletown. From Middletown the route followed the valley of the Juniata for 172 miles. From Hollidaysburg, the Allegheny Portage Railroad ran to Johnstown, and from there, again by canal and river, 104 miles to Pittsburgh. The route was, in short, a bit of a mess, with the Appalachian Mountains preventing anything like a direct route from Harrisburg to Pittsburg.

On December 10, 1852, rail lines had been completed from both ends of the Allegheny Portage

connecting Philadelphia and Pittsburgh. By 1858, the Pennsylvania had purchased the state railroads.

The development of the Pennsylvania in the years following included construction and the purchase, acquisition or leasing of a number of other lines. The Camden and Amboy Railroad had begun with a line between Bordentown and Hitestown, New Jersey, in 1832, and in 1834 had a line from Amboy to Camden. The New Jersey Railroad meanwhile, in 1834, operated a line from the Hudson River to Elizabeth. These two roads were later merged as the United Railroads, and by 1871 the Pennsylvania had leased them in order to have a connection with New York. In 1869, the Pennsylvania leased the Pittsburgh, Fort Wayne and Chicago Railroad, and in 1864 had leased the Philadelphia and Erie Railroad. Other roads in which the Pennsylvania obtained a controlling interest included the Northern Central Railroad, the Long Island Railroad, the Philadelphia, Wilmington and Baltimore Railroad, the Madison and Indianapolis, the Steubenville and Indiana, the Indianapolis and St. Louis, the Vandalia, the West Jersey and Seashore, and others. Through all of them, the Pennsylvania was able to serve a greater and greater area of the East and Mid-West.

The Pennsylvania was the first railroad to use steel tracks, having imported a quantity from Bessemer in England in England in 1863. Through the use of steel rails, it was possible to carry much greater loads per axle, and there was an even more important advantage in the superior wearing quality and safety of such rails. The use of track tanks for picking up water for the locomotives while the train is in motion was another of the Pennsylvania's innovations, being first employed as early as 1870.

The main line construction of the Pennsylvania was a remarkable feat of engineering, requiring the bridging of the Susquehanna, passage over the Horseshoe Curve, through the tunnel at Gallitzin, along the Conemaugh River, and the tunnels under the Hudson and East Rivers. The Susquehanna bridge was the largest stone arch bridge in the world, with four tracks crossing on 49 arches for a length of 3850 feet over the river.

In 1910, the tunnels under the North and East Rivers were officially opened, permitting access to the new Pennsylvania station in New York City, construction of which had been started in 1904. In later years, the construction of the Hell Gate bridge between Long Island and New York City was another task of considerable engineering importance conceived by the Pennsylvania.

In 1869, a Pennsylvania train was outfitted with air brakes. Previous to the development of air brakes by George Westinghouse, train cars had to be laboriously stopped with hand brakes. The practical air brake system was probably the single most important safety development in the history of railroading. The Altoona shops of the Pennsylvania-- where numerous advances in brake design were made--were, in themselves, an interesting story, being the largest group of railroad shops in the world, comprising 125 buildings and over 218 acres of trackage. A locomotive testing plant which had been on exhibit at the St. Louis exposition in 1904 was moved to Altoona at the end of the exposition and was the first equipment of its type by which the performance of locomotives could be carefully analyzed.

The Pennsylvania eventually became famous during the steam era for its deluxe passenger trains, such as the "Broadway Limited," noted for fast schedule between New York and Chicago, the "Congressional Limited," the "Spirit of St. Louis," the "Red Arrow," the "Jeffersonian," the "Trail Blazer," the "Silver Meteor," the "Champion," and the "Southerner."

The Union Pacific Railroad began as a result of one of the most significant transportation projects in American history: the decision to fund a trans-continental railroad linking the East and West coasts of the United States.

On the morning of May 10, 1869, the driving of the golden spike at Promontory, Utah, united the Union Pacific and Central Pacific railroads into the first transcontinental railroad. Two small rails of steel stretched across the endless miles of prairie, laid unballasted on a fresh grade through the vast territory of western United States. Having just passed the crucial days of the Civil War, this opening of a new frontier made possible in a practical sense the economic development of the western states of the young country.

Averaging twenty miles per hour, wood-burning steam locomotives pulled wooden cars over the rails, bringing settlers to enlarge those towns already established during its construction. Other settlers turned the virgin sod of the prairie to cultivate farms and transform the region into the granary of the world.

From the single line of a little more than 1,000 miles at the time of the driving of the golden spike in 1869, the Union Pacific grew rapidly until it consisted of over 7,500 miles of main lines and branches thirty years later. Ultimately, the Union Pacific had a line extending into the states of the Pacific Northwest with its rich timberland and a short line extended southward through Utah pointed at Los Angeles, accomplished in 1903.

By then the Union Pacific had assumed final outlines, with a main line from Omaha to Ogden and Salt Lake City, Utah, with connections over the Chicago and North Western to Chicago and over the Southern Pacific (the old Central Pacific) to San Francisco. From Kansas City another main line continued to Denver with a connection to Cheyenne and the original line. The main line to the Pacific Northwest extended from Wyoming, with branches throughout the state, and the line south from Salt Lake City ran all the way through to Los Angeles and Southern California.

An ad from the second world war is shown opposite. This ad features the "Big Boy" engine made by Alco. A card on the same engine from the Union Pacific, left, is also shown.

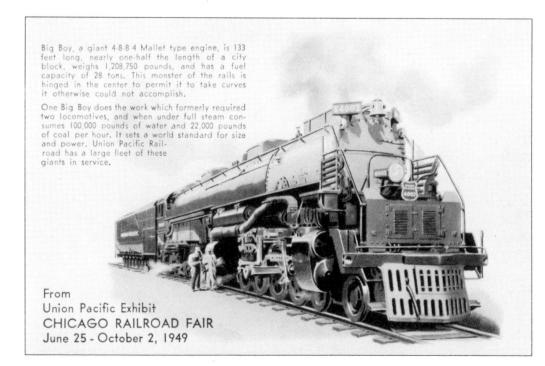

Big Boy, a giant 4-8-8-4 Mallet type engine, is 133 feet long, nearly one-half the length of a city block, weighs 1,208,750 pounds, and has a fuel capacity of 28 tons. This monster of the rails is hinged in the center to permit it to take curves it otherwise could not accomplish.

One Big Boy does the work which formerly required two locomotives, and when under full steam consumes 100,000 pounds of water and 22,000 pounds of coal per hour. It sets a world standard for size and power. Union Pacific Railroad has a large fleet of these giants in service.

From
Union Pacific Exhibit
CHICAGO RAILROAD FAIR
June 25 - October 2, 1949

156

AMERICA IN MOTION.... by Lowell Thomas
News summary from national arsenal of mobile power

I'VE SEEN a locomotive over 130 feet long, speeding war material over mountain grades, and I'll never forget it! Now I'm here where 20 of them were born...the home of "The Big Boys," 7,000 horse-power, the heaviest and most powerful locomotives ever made...and I know now that some of the tanks and gun carriages on that train were made right here, side by side with "Big Boy."

I'VE WATCHED troops unloading from train after train, powered by fast Diesel or Steam-Liners. And now I understand how the railroads are able to handle this big job, biggest in history, so well. Here they build the most modern, streamlined locomotives in the world, both steam and diesel-powered. Build them fast. Build them to meet special wartime requirements. Build them to win.

I'VE FELT all along that power to produce is our greatest asset. But I never saw a speed-up so swift or so well directed as this. Men swarming all over a Diesel-Locomotive, building medium tanks... forging big-gun parts... skilled man-power under experienced directions. We Americans, we expect miracles. And by George, we get them!

I ASKED about power, and I got my answer in terms of diesels for the Navy ...Diesel or Steam-Liners for the railroads, whichever is needed to do a particular job best...tanks and gun carriages for the Army ...power to turn the tide of war against any enemy. A great country, this. And something I saw here tells me we're going to keep it that way.

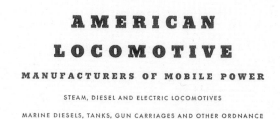

AMERICAN LOCOMOTIVE
MANUFACTURERS OF MOBILE POWER

STEAM, DIESEL AND ELECTRIC LOCOMOTIVES

MARINE DIESELS, TANKS, GUN CARRIAGES AND OTHER ORDNANCE

APPENDIX I
Origins of the Steam Locomotive

(Many organizations of professional railroad men appeared in the heyday of steam. Railroad executives, suppliers, designers and lay enthusiasts joined such groups and gathered regularly to discuss and debate railroad topics. Formal presentations were likely to be fairly esoteric--"The Theory and Practice of Railroad Equipment Painting," to cite one actual example-- but once in a while a topic fascinating to the lay enthusiast would come along. Such an occasion occurred at the New England Railroad Club on the evening of January 14, 1902. Angus Sinclair, the noted 19th Century railroad engineer and writer--a man who witnessed first hand with an expert's eye the development of the railroads--gave an historic lecture on the development of the steam locomotive. To our knowledge, this is the first time this document has been printed for general distribution. ED.)

Easy means of intercommunication have been properly valued by all nations and races that have ever made material progress in civilization. Lord Bacon says that "there are three things which make a nation great and prosperous--a fertile soil, busy workshops, and easy conveyance of men and commodities from place to place."

When the idea of applying the potential power of steam to lighten the drudgery of mankind was little more than a philosopher's dream, when a practical steam engine was only a hope, its most useful field was by many considered to be in carrying heavy burdens and in bringing distant places in to closer connection.

The need of improved methods of transportation did not, however, produce the steam engine. Grim necessity brought it forth when great properties were falling into ruin, because animal power was incompetent to concentrate great effort in limited space. The steam engine was invented when horses could no longer do the work of pumping water out of valuable mines 500 feet deep. It was a foregone conclusion that the steam engine would be applied to locomotive purposes as soon as increase of business rendered the horse unequal to the task of supplying motive power on roads and canals.

After a practicable steam engine was put in operation, it took half a century to develop it into a motor suitable for driving manufacturing machinery. Another half century passed before inventors began attempting to experiment on the building of an engine that could be used to drive a vehicle on land. Farseeing, progressive men, who kept informed on leading scientific achievements, were convinced that steam locomotion would come in to existence when sufficiently urgent necessity would cause its birth. A variety of experimental locomotives had been built or patented before the eighteenth century closed, but nothing of a promising nature was produced until in 1803 Richard Trevithick, a Cornish mine captain and engineer, applied a steam engine to a carriage which ran successfully on common roads. Richard Trevithick was an inventive genius, and his work exerted powerful influence in the producing of a successful locomotive engine.

Inventors in various countries now began to interest themselves in designing engines suitable for land transportation; but it was not until 1827 that an engine was built which did work on a railroad at decidedly lower cost than animal power.

When the nineteenth century began, Great Britain, more than any other country, needed the use of the steam engine for help in land transportation; but the century had not passed over two decades when the United States was becoming as urgently in need of locomotives as Great Britain was. But the British Isles was well provided with mechanics who worked in iron and other metals, and naturally numerous attempts were made there to design a locomotive that would take the place of horses. There were mines, especially collieries, where tramways were in use to provide easy movement of wheeled vehicles then operated by horses, and every tramway stood inviting the steam engine.

The first engine made to run on rails and haul cars regularly was built in 1813 by William Hedley and Timothy Hackworth. They imitated engines previously designed by Trevithick, but their first engine was not a success. A second one was built which worked fairly well, and is now to be seen in South Kensington Museum, London, bearing the name of "Puffing Billy."

George Stephenson was employed at a neighboring colliery, and he built a locomotive a year later imitating Hedley's engine as closely as he could, but his engine proved next to a failure. The building of locomotives was, however, now fairly begun, and quite a number were built and put to work by various makers during the next twelve years; but they were all very unsatisfactory, for their work of hauling coal cars was about as costly as the use of horses. The high-pressure steam engine was strange to the English engineers, and they heaped blunder upon blunder in applying it to a moveable carriage.

Before the introduction of the locomotive, barely all steam engines in Europe had vertical cylinders, and the first designers of locomotives naturally followed the practice that had found favor with the steam engines that were doing satisfactory work. This led to a long train of complications, and greatly increased the difficulties of building a locomotive that could do its work without breakage. The history of the locomotive from the time Hedley built his "Puffing Billy," in 1814, up to 1829 is a record of disasters, failures, and of men's perseverance while in the grasp of distressing discouragements. About the beginning of the latter year, designers began to try cylinders located so that the piston's connection could be attached directly to the driving wheels. This did away with the

intervention of walking beams, gearing, or other complex appliances that were much used on the earlier engines.

Hedley's "Puffing Billy" was the beginning of a type that became the prevailing fashion up to the time when the dirctors of the Liverpool & Manchester Railway, in 1829, offered a prize of 500 pounds ($2,500) for the most successful locomotive. Hedley's engine was not a model of simplicity, but its complications were modest compared to many of its successors. The pioneer locomotive builders did not realize that complicated mechanism was objectionable until sad experience with breakdowns taught them that the fewer parts used which were not liable to breakage, the more successful the engine was likely to be. They were the engineers who first learned about the extra destructive effects that result from an engine jolting over a rough track. Their predecessors had to deal only with machines secured to a solid foundation, where complication of parts was of little consequence.

Most people in this country, who know a little about early railroad history, imagine that Stephenson's "Rocket," which won the 500 pound prize at the Rainhill competition, held in 1829, was the first locomotive introduced on railroads, and that it left the makers' hands a perfect motor to become a pattern for all other practical locomotives. This is a popular mistake. There were probably fifty locomotives at work in different parts of England before the "Rocket" became famous. One railway, the Stockton & Darlington, twenty-five miles long, was opened for business in 1825, and was operated by locomotives built by the Stephensons in their machine shops erected in Newcastle the previous year, the first of them having been "Locomotion." The engines were far from being satisfactory; for eighteen months after the road was opened the directors seriously thought of substituting horses, for a report made to them indicated that operating with locomotives cost more than horse power.

At this junction Timothy Hackworth, who was manager of the railroad and was one of the best mechanics and engine builders in Great Britain, offered to build an engine which he guaranteed would do the work cheaper than horses. His offer was accepted and he built the "Royal George," which was a six-coupled engine with vertical cylinders. The engine did the work well and redeemed the waning reputation of the locomotive.

Hackworth had been foreman blacksmith at the works where Hedley was superintendent, and he helped to build "Puffing Billy," much of the work having been done by himself. He was first superintendent of Stephenson's works in Newcastle, and the engine called "Locomotion," which was called George Stephenson's first successful locomotive, was built under Hackworth's supervision. Those who have most carefully studied the early history of the locomotive claim that Hackworth deserved the credit of first making the locomotive engine a success.

In spite of the success of the "Royal George" and of others afterwards put to work on the same line, the upper class of engineers were not convinced that locomotives were satisfactory as motive power. A year after the "Royal George" was put to work, two of the most eminent engineers in the British Isles were engaged to report on what would be the best motive power for the Liverpool and Manchester Railway, then nearly ready for opening, and they reported in favor of stationary engines and rope traction. George Stephenson was chief engineer of the road, and he fought vigorously in favor of locomotives, and his persistence led the directors to offer the prize for the best locomotive already referred to. Five engines were entered, and three of them demonstrated that locomotive traction was practicable. The successful engine was the "Rocket," which made George Stephenson famous.

George Stephenson receives the credit of being the inventor of the locomotive, but when the work he did is closely analyzed we find that no proof exists of Stephenson having invented anything that improved the locomotive. He was deficient in inventive attributes, but he had the faculty of knowing a good thing when he saw it, and he perceived that railroads would at some time become the principal means of land transportation.

He also clearly perceived that some form of portable steam engine would be the future motive power of railroads. Stephenson was a good representative of the best type of Englishman. Opinionated, and ever pushing his opinions with bull dog tenacity, he made weaker minds yield before his views on railways and locomotives. This was his hobby, and he rode it so furiously that the British world was drawn along often against its will. By his dominating will, persistent determination and forcible arguments, he prevailed on British capitalists to construct a railway for general transportation, and forced them to try locomotives when all the scientific world was against him. He gave his country the honor of originating steam-operated railways at the moment when America was almost ready to grasp the prize.

With the successful opening of the Liverpool & Manchester Railway, public opinion, which previously had been very sceptical about the utility of railway enterprise, suddenly turned in the other direction, and frantic demand for railways arose from nearly every community. The demand for railway construction became a mania which floated many rotten schemes and ended in one of the worst panics Britain had ever known. Within the next decade thirty-six railway companies were operating track, and about 1,430 miles of railway, mostly double track, had been built. This was extraordinary progress considering the delays that the law imposes before a company can begin to build a railway in the United Kingdom.

The establishing of locomotive building works more than kept pace with railway construction. The owners of nearly every machine shop of any consequence was prepared to build locomotives, and during the first decade after the Liverpool & Manchester Railway was opened, hundreds of locomotives were set to work, many of them being fearful and wonderful specimens. This was the freak period of locomotive construction in the British Isles, but from among the curiosities permanent types were gradually evolved.

The use of vertical cylinders was soon abandoned, first in favor of inclined cylinders similar to those used on the "Rocket," and a little later for horizontal cylinders, either inside or outside of the frames. It was strange that vertical cylinders were not abandoned sooner, for they could not be used on the rough track of the pioneer tramways and railways without great piston clearance to prevent striking the heads, for the distance between the cylinder and the axle often varied several inches, due to the vertical motion caused by the rough track. This made upright cylinder engines very wasteful of fuel.

About the beginning of the railway era, a locomotive called the "Liverpool," Fig. 1, was built by Edward Bury, which exercised a wonderful influence on American locomotive designing. It

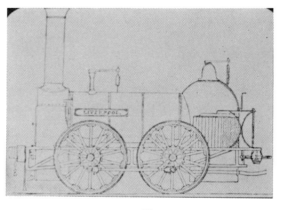

Fig.1

was a four-wheel coupled engine and had inside cylinders, bar frames inside of the wheels, and a haystack (hemispherical) firebox boiler. The inside cylinder arrangement appealed to the engineering acumen of Robert Stephenson, and he began to build engines with the cylinders below the smokebox, a move which exerted great influence in making the inside cylinder locomotive the favorite type in the British Isles. The bar frame did not long find favor with British locomotive designers. They preferred plates that required no welding; but early American locomotive builders were impressed by the simplicity of the bar frame, and it gradually became standard on this continent. Very few British locomotive builders, except Gooch of the Great Western, used the Bury boiler, but it found much favor with our pioneer railroad mechanics and was used until years of hard service demonstrated that

the hemispherical firebox was not adapted for large boilers.

The first inside connected engine built by Robert Stephenson was called the "Planet," which resembled Bury's Liverpool, but had a single pair of driving wheels and outside frames. It worked so well that it became the representative of a class which was largely imitated. Many of the early engines built by the Stephenson works for this country were of the "Planet" type, the "John Bull," the first engine used by the Camden & Amboy, the oldest stem of the great Pennsylvania Railroad system, having been one of them.

The "Planet" was notable as having been the first locomotive built with otuside frames. These were rather peculiar, for they were put below the driving axle, the jaws for the axle box extending upwards. That arrangement was not repeated, but the outside frame suited English ideas, and it gradually grew into favor until it became used on all their railways, until the inside plate frame became more popular for powerful engines.

The works of Robert Stephenson & Co., Newcastle, England, built a great many locomotives which were sold to American railroad companies, and there is a belief prevailing that George Stephenson was the builder. This is a mistake. Robert Stephenson, the son of George, was in charge of the works,and whatever special engineering features were put upon the engines were due to Robert Stephenson's engineering ability.

Among the curiosities built during the first railway decade was Roberts' "Experiment," which had upright cylinders and transmitted the power by means of a bell crank. This experiment was not successful. The engine is, however, worthy of mention, because it was the first locomotive built with piston valves. The valves were of ingenious design, but they proved no better than the ball crank, and were soon abandoned. An improved form of this engine is shown in Fig. 2. It was built for a Scotch railway, where I received the first rudiments of an engineer's training, and did good work.

Up to 1840 nearly all British locomotives were carried on four wheels, most of them having

Fig. 2

Fig. 3

one pair of driving wheels, and one pair of small carriers. With the opening of the Great Western Railway in 1838, which had a track gauge of seven feet, a demand for heavier locomotives arose, and six wheel engines became common. About this time the movement in favor of huge driving wheels originated, and Fig. 3 shows one of the first engines built for the Great Western. Besides the immense driving wheels, which were 10 feet in diameter, this engine had the first wind splitting device applied to a locomotive. Great things were expected of this means of reducing wind resistance, but the only result was disappointment. There were three of these engines, and they had cylinders 14x20 inches. The boiler pressure was about 70 pounds to the square inch. The tractive power was about 2,000 pounds, sufficient only to start about 130 tons under favorable conditions.

British locomotive engineers have always displayed a strong predilection for big driving wheels. Some of the early Great Western locomotives were geared to make the driving wheels equivalent to eighteen feet diameter. The purpose of

this style of design was to reduce the piston speed to the lowest practical limits, with the idea that the steam economy would be increased. The famous engineer, D.K. Clark, exploded this theory, but big driving wheels have always been popular in Europe, especially in Great Britain.

Inside cylinder engines became popular for two leading reasons. One was that the cylinders were protected in the smoke box from chilling influences, the other was that an inside connected engine rode steadier than one with outside cylinders in the days prior to the use of counterbalanced driving wheels. The Stephensons built one engine with three cylinders, two outside the frames and one inside, the purpose being to remedy the sinuous (nosing) motion of outside cylinder engines; but the effect was not so good as counterbalance weights, which were introduced a few years later. During the development of the locomotive after driving-wheel counterbalance weights had come into use, engines with outside cylinders became favorites with many railway men, owing to the convenience of getting at the working parts; but hard service indicated that outside cylinders could not be secured so rigidly to plate frames as inside cylinders which are securely bolted together or cast in one piece, and from this cause the outside connected engine has been falling into disrepute for several years.

In the early railway days a locomotive was built in England which we would class among the freaks, yet it exerted great influence. This was the "Crampton" engine, Fig. 4. The engine did not accord with British taste, but it became very popular with Frenchmen, and became, to a great extent, the prototype of the French passenger engine. The plate shown represents a modern engine still in service on the Eastern Railway of France.

The lines of development for passenger service in Great Britain settled down for years upon single driver engines, with drivers in the middle and carrying wheels in front and behind. After the introduction of the American style of carriages, many locomotive superintendents began to use four-coupled engines with four-wheel truck, but express engines with a single pair of drivers are still popular on several railways.

For freight service six-coupled engines without any truck became the favorite, and engines of that design are found on nearly every railway in the British Isles. Within the last three years the agitation in favor of American methods has brought

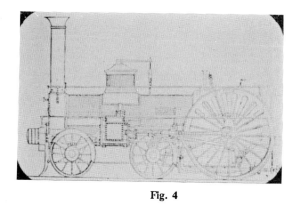

Fig. 4

forth some eight-coupled freight engines, and the tendency is now in that direction.

The agitation in favor of railroad building began in the United States about the same time as it began in Great Britain, and the machinery for operating them was developed largely by native engineers. Thanks to ignorant writers for encyclopedias and to writers of romancing biography, there is an impression prevailing that American railroad pioneers were guided entirely by English types of machinery and English methods of construction, which is a fallacy. Those who have studied the subject thoroughly believe that railroads and locomotive building in America would not have been much delayed had Watt never worked on improving the steam engine, and had George Stephenson never been born. Oliver Evans, a native of Delaware, developed the high-pressure high-speed engine as an improvement on Newcomen's atmosphere engine, and it was much better adapted for locomotive purposes than the ponderous slow-moving engines that early British inventors had to work after while designing locomotives.

Americans, as a rule, knew very little about what Englishmen had done when they began building railroads, and their first locomotives were purely original. Very little accurate information had reached America concerning what had been done in England before our people entered earnestly into the building of railroads. Before the railroad era there was scarcely any means of spreading scientific information, and few Englishmen knew anything about how railways were going to be operated when the Liverpool & Manchester Railway was under construction. Six months before the railway was ready for opening, the directors were inundated with schemes for operating the road. There were plans proposed for working the cars by water power. Some proposed hydrogen, others carbonic acid gas. Atmospheric pressure had its advocates; other favored greased cog rails. There was a multitude of counsellors who proved nothing except that even the scientific men of England had no knowledge of what had been done by Trevithick, by Hedley, Stephenson, Hackworth, and others.

That being the condition of engineering knowledge in Great Britain, it was not surprising that Americans had to fall back upon their own resources when they proceeded to build railroads and to put them into operation. The nation has always been celebrated for self reliance, and the pioneer railroad builders pushed along without hesitation, crossing the bridges of difficulty when they were reached. So far were they guiltless of imitating English methods that they built and began operating the first railroad in the world ever projected for general traffic. That was the Baltimore & Ohio Railroad, which was chartered in 1827 and part opened for business in 1830.

The road was very crooked, and there were grave doubts that locomotives could be made to pass the curves, so horses were employed at first. But Peter Cooper, afterwards celebrated as the great philanthropist who gave the Cooper Union for industrial purposes in New York, believed that locomotives could be built that would operate the road, and to prove the faith that was in him built a small engine which proved that his idea was correct.

Cooper's engine was the "Tom Thumb," Fig. 5, a remarkably tiny locomotive with one upright cylinder 3-1/4 x 14-1/2 inches, and an upright boiler having tubes made from gun barrels.

Draft for the fire was maintained by a revolving fan. It performed the duties for which the engine was built, most of them having been of a missionary character. It proved that steam power could be used to operate the Baltimore & Ohio Railroad, and revived the spirits of the promoters of the enterprise, who were becoming despondent about the prospects of the property. The "Tom Thumb" was little bigger than a modern hand car and was only about 1-1/2 horse-power, but its design seems to have exerted considerable influence on our early locomotives.

Cooper's engine was not actually the first locomotive to turn a wheel on an American railroad, but it was the first successful machine. The Delaware & Hudson Canal Co. built a piece of railroad which they wished to operate by steam power, and they sent one of their engineers, Horatio Allen, to purchase locomotives suitable for doing the work. He bought an engine called the "Stourbridge Lion," which resembled Stephenson's

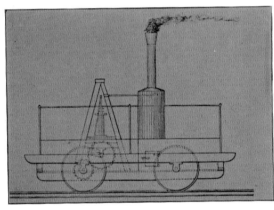

Fig. 5

"Locomotion." It made a few trips on the railroad near Honesdale, Pa., but was declared a failure and abandoned. It exerted no influence on American locomotive building or design.

The sentiment in favor of railroad building developed very rapidly in the United States after the shortcomings of canals had been plainly demonstrated. The men who took the lead in advocating railroads were the most influential and intelligent men in the country, having clear views about what they wanted. When DeWitt Clinton, in

1812, was urging through the New York legislature the act for the construction of the Erie Canal, Colonel Stevens of Hoboken insisted that he could build a railroad on which cars would be drawn by steam locomotives at a cheaper rate, and at a much higher speed than canal boats. He submitted particulars of his plans, and they did not differ much from the railroads that were subsequently built.

Oliver Evans had a clear idea of what his high-speed engine was destined to accomplish in transportation and urged the building of railroads. He predicted that railroads would yet be built on which his style of engine would haul trains, which would enable passengers to leave Washington in the morning, dine in Philadelphia, and sup in New York.

Shortly after the experiments with Peter Cooper's model locomotive, the management of the Baltimore & Ohio advertised, offering a premium of $500 for a locomotive, built in the United States, which would draw fifteen tons gross weight at fifteen miles an hour. In due time this offer brought to the company five locomotives, all built at different places, all different in design, and none of them imitating British models. One was a rotary engine. The preference was given to an engine built by Davis and Gartner, of York, Pa. The engine had a vertical boiler of a curious, original pattern, and upright cylinders. She did not work very satisfactorily. The experience with this engine led to the building of the "Atlantic," Fig. 6, which was designed by Phineas Davis and Ross Winans, who was assistant engineer of machinery of the Baltimore & Ohio. The "Atlantic," which became known as the beginning of the "Grasshopper" type, had a vertical boiler with a fan for stimulating the fire. The cylinders were vertical, 10x20 inches, and they transmitted the power to a supplementary driving shaft by means of spur and pinion, which were geared up to make the wheels revolve twice for every turn of the crank. By this means, wheels three feet in diameter were made equivalent to driving wheels six feet in diameter.

About twenty engines of the "Atlantic" type were built, and they worked very successfully in developing railroad traffic, and only went out of favor when engines with a longer wheel base became necessary. Some "Grasshoppers" were used about Mount Clare shops till six or seven years ago. These engines filled a gap in railroad operating, but they exerted little influence on locomotive development more than warning designers against upright cylinders and upright boilers. They were, however, an excellent object

Fig. 6

lesson of difficulties that could be overcome by intelligence and perseverance. The United States was, in 1830, almost purely an agricultural country, yet, with few mechanics skilled in the working of metals, and very meagre workshop facilities, the people began the work of locomotive building in a spirit thatguaranteed success.

In describing the Baltimore & Ohio locomotives, I have reached out a little ahead of the story. For years there had been much agitation in Charleston, S.C., for the building of a railroad that would extend 136 miles to Hamburg in the western part of the State. The enterprising citizens of Charleston aimed to capture the shipment of cotton which was drifting to other harbors.

The South Carolina Railroad Company was chartered in 1828. The promoters of the enterprise appeared to be wonderfully energetic men, for they lost no time in pushing the work of construction, and part of the road was ready for opening in 1830.

Shortly after the company was formed, Horatio Allen, who brought the "Stourbridge Lion" from England, was appointed chief engineer. By his advice the road was built to be suitable for

locomotives as motive power. Mr. E.L. Miller, a citizen of Charleston, who took great interest in the railroad, offered to have a locomotive built which would operate the road satisfactorily, and his offer was accepted. He had the engine built at the West Point foundry, New York. The work was done so expeditiously that the engine was taken to Charleston and went into service in October, 1830. The engine, which was called "The Best Friend," is shown in Fig. 7.

The success of Cooper's "Tom Thumb" had prejudiced people in favor of upright boilers, and accordingly the "Best Friend" had that kind of a steam generator. The engine had inclined cylinders and two pairs of coupled wheels. The boiler was secured between the frames at one end, and the cylinders and water tank were secured at the other end. This locomotive was distinctly original in design and worked well until the negro fireman, annoyed by the steam escaping from the safety valve, weighted the lever, with the result that the boiler exploded. "West Point," was under construction. It had a horizontal boiler and inclined cylinders set alongside the firebox. The frames were wood plated with iron, and they were inside the driving wheels.

There appeared to be no difficulty in finding men who could design practical locomotives, but the shops that could build them were scarce. When the South Carolina Railroad was finished from Charleston to Hamburg, it was the longest railroad in the world. The third locomotive built for it was designed by Horatio Allen and was a double-ended freak that made no history. The next

Fig. 7

one was built by Mr. Baldwin in 1834, and was called the "E.L. Miller," Fig. 8. This engine, as will be noticed, had a single pair of drivers set behind the firebox, which was of the Bury type, and a four-wheel truck in front. The cylinders were set close to the smokebox inside the frames and transmitted the power to half-crank axles invented by the builder.

This type of engine, with various modifications, became highly popular on American railroads, and was the form from which the modern locomotive was developed. A great many experiments were made with curious forms of engines, but these were the product of original thought searching for the fittest forms.

The decidedly experimental period of our locomotive history was the first railroad decade from 1830 to 1840. During that time many locomotives were produced which are now interesting as illustrations of blunders and products of fallacies. But they were the mistakes that made pitfalls on the highway that leads to success. This decade is celebrated for the bold experiments made for the purpose of improving the locomotive. The crank is in evidence occasionally, but most of the off forms produced were mistakes made by

Fig. 8

practical men.

The first important improvement effected upon the locomotive during the decade under discussion was the four-wheel engine truck introduced by John B. Jervis, chief engineer of the Mohawk & Hudson Railroad. It was applied to an engine called the "Experiment," built at the West Point Foundry in 1831. The New York Central people are very proud of the "DeWitt Clinton" which was the first engine used on what was the first link of their system, but the "Experiment" was an engine of much greter importance on the development of railroad motive power.

In 1840 there were about 270 locomotives working in the United States on fifty-six railroads that were partly finished; but the greater part of the mileage was still operated by horses. The length of the track in operation was about 2,700 miles. It may appear strange that so many locomotives were employed and yet performed only part of the work. This happened because the mileage was cut up into many small sections, because the engines were small, and because they were carefully coddled by the men in charge. On some of the roads engines were not taken out in stormy weather. Horses had to pull the cars at such times.

The scarcity of mechanics in the United States, and of machine shops with facilities for building locomotives, led to the importing of a great many locomotives, most of them having come from the shops of Robert Stephenson & Co., Newcastle, England. A few were built by Bury and other British engine builders. The foreign built locomotives now began to exert a decided influence on American designs, but none of it was lasting except the bar frame, which was borrowed from the Bury engines. The hemispherical firebox of the same builder became a favorite with American locomotive builders, and remained popular for about twenty years. It was used by Baldwin and Winans and Norris and Eastwick and Harrison till about 1848, and Rogers used it as late as 1854.

The first general movement made to improve the American locomotive was the extension of the wheel base of the engine. The principal aim of this improvement was to distribute the weight over the track; for although the engines were light, the rails were relatively lighter, and great care was necessary to prevent the wheels damaging the iron straps fastened to stringers, which did duty as rails on most of the railroads. John B. Jervis originated this movement in a practical way when he put a four-wheel truck under the front of the "Experiment." It was found by experience that lengthening the wheel base greatly improved the riding of the engine. This was very important, for the men who road upon the engines were influential individuals; and partly through their influence the four-wheel engines imported were nearly all quickly changed, and a truck put under the front end.

During the decade from 1830 to 1840 most railroads had settled down to the use of the six-wheel engine, which had the truck in front and a pair of single drivers behind, similar to the "E.L. Miller," but experimental engines were quite common. There were differences even in the six-wheel engine, for Baldwin placed the drivers behind the firebox, while Norris placed them in front. These were at first the two principal locomotive builders, and there was considerable rivalry between them, principally as to who could build the best working engine. This was the beginning of the rivalry betwen our locomotive builders, which has been kept up to the present generation. Railroad men have always taken sides in this rivalry, which was violently active at some periods. To listen to the round-house talk about engines of different makes, one might conclude that certain engines hauled two or three cars with the name-plates alone.

As the country prospered, stimulated by railroad operating and railroad building, the need for heavier locomotives gradually became urgent. Robert L. Stevens, who was chief engineer in the construction of the Camden & Amboy Railroad, had invented the T rail, about 1831, and it began gradually to displace the strap rail. With the introduction of stronger rails railroad managers kept calling for heavier engines, a demand that has gone on steadily ever since. The first practical answer to this demand was the inventing, in 1836, by Henry Campbell, chief engineer of the Philadelphia & Germantown Railroad, of an eight-wheel engine having two pairs of driving wheels connected and a four-wheel truck. This engine was the prototype of the far-famed "American" locomotive.

An engine designed according to Campbell's plans was built and did fairly well, but was hard riding and did not advance the type in popularity. The engine lacked an essential feature. There were no equalizers between the drivers, and

nothing but the ordinary springs over each driving box to transmit the weight.

A new locomotive firm, Eastwick & Harrison, began operations in Philadelphia early in the thirties, and they soon began to display both originality and enterprise in their designs. In the same year that Campbell's eight-wheel engine was built, Eastwick & Harrison constructed an eight-wheel engine called the "Mercury," which had the driving axles running in a separate square frame connected to the main frame above it by a single central bearing on each side. This engine made a step towards equalizing beams.

In 1839 Eastwick & Harrison received an order from the Reading for a big engine to weigh eleven tons. The first engine built on this order was the "Gowan & Marx," Fig. 9. This engine made fortunes for its builders.

The engine was four-wheel connected, and equalizing levers were placed between the drivers, invented and patented by Joseph Harrison, Jr., the previous year. The boiler was of the Bury type, and the fire box was five feet long, which was then considered something gigantic. Two-inch tubes were used, and they nearly filled the barrel of the boiler, but were only five feet long.

The cylinders were 12-1/2 x 18 inches, and the driving wheels were 42 inches outside diameter. With 100 pounds boiler pressure the engine had about 3,000 pounds tractive power, which was regarded as enormous at that time.

It will be noticed that the engine had bar-frames after the Bury style, and in this was a pioneer of what became a standard form. Very soon after being put to work the engine became famous for the great tractive power it developed, and its extraordinary capacity for hauling heavy trains. On its trial in 1840 the engine hauled one hundred and four four-wheel cars of coal from Reading to Philadelphia at the rate of 9.82 miles per hour. The road had a falling gradient of nearly four feet per mile, 27 miles level, 9 miles at one place, and only one ascending grade of 26 feet per mile for 2,100 feet. The train weighed 423 tons and, including weight of tender, equalled forty times the weight of the engine. Nothing near that tractive power had

Fig. 9

previously been made, and it is hard to excel today.

This feat of the Gowan & Marx was heralded at home and abroad, and the Emperor of Russia sent two officials to report upon American railroad machinery and our methods of operating railroads. It resulted in Eastwick & Harrison being invited by the Russian government to establish locomotive building works in St. Petersburg which they accepted, and made a big fortune.

Eastwick & Harrison introduced several improvements. Besides first using the weight-equalizing beam, they brought the blower into use and the crude beginning of a locomotive cab. They designed the first quartering machine, and put upon their engines a variety of conveniences that became permanent attachments.

Among those who were laboring most zealously at this time to improve the locomotive, Mr. Baldwin took a leading part. He did not like Campbell's idea of connecting four wheels on a rigid base, but he introduced a six-wheel connected engine with four wheels in front, forming a flexible truck. These engines became very popular for

Fig. 10

freight service. A modification of it was made for passenger service in which a small pair of wheels were used in front, and the flexible truck for the drivers. As demands for faster passenger engines arose, he introduced the type shown in Fig. 10. This served until Mr. Baldwin became convinced that his objections to the Campbell type were not well founded. After that he fell into line as a builder of the eight-wheel American engine.

A man who put an indelible mark upon the American locomotive and performed most valuable services in developing railroad motive power was Ross Winans of Baltimore. I left him as assistant chief mechanical engineer helping to improve the "Grasshopper" engine. He afterwards left railroad service to become a locomotive builder. He improved the "Grasshopper" by applying horizontal cylinders. Trainmen even at that early date were given to naming types of engines to fit their ideas as to the eternal fitness of things. They called the metamorphosed "Grasshopper" a "Crab."

The "Crab" represented progress, but the railroads of Pennsylvania and Maryland were frequently congested with coal that was delayed for want of motive power. Winans perceived that much heavier engines were necessary, and in trying to produce something that would provide what was needed, he designed and built an eight-wheel connected engine, which the trainmen promptly named the "Mud Digger." All the weight of the engine rested upon the driving wheels, and it was really the first eight-wheel connected locomotive ever built in America, and although unsatisfactory in some respects led the way to other eight-wheel connected engines. The "Mud Digger," whose proper name was the "Buffalo," was a development of Winans "Crab" type. It had a vertical boiler, but the cylinders were horizontal and transmitted the power through a supplementary driving shaft that operated the driving axle through spur gearing. It was an over-grown crab.

Winans next venture of an original character was for the Reading. It was called the "Delaware" and had eight wheels connected direct and a horizontal boiler with a Bury firebox. This was the first engine belonging to the Reading which burned

Fig.11

anthracite coal, those previously used having burned wood in hauling coal to the market.

The B. & O. people were finding out that the vertical boiler was not well adapted to locomotive service, so in 1848 Winans built for them his first camel, shown in Fig. 11. This type became the standard freight engine of the road and was in use for many years. All that it needed to be made a consolidation engine was a pony truck in front.

About 1846 Mr. Baldwin began building eight-wheel connected engines for freight service, and they became very popular with the coal roads and others having heavy freight business. They had the flexible four-wheeldriving-wheel truck in front and two pairs of driving wheels behind, the whole of them coupled. Only the working out of a few details were necessary to provide the railroad world with a modern freight engine.

Fig. 12 is the first ten-wheel engine in America, and was built about 1848 by Septamus Norris for the Reading Railroad. James Milholland was at that time superintendent of motive power of

Fig.12

the Reading, and was a very enterprising improver of the locomotive, and put his mark upon the early engines as strongly as any of our pioneer engineers. This engine burned anthracite coal, and was the first of a class of very successful engines which were built under Milholland's directions.

Rogers, Ketchum & Grosvenor began building locomotives in 1837, and their first engine, the "Sandusky," had a four-wheel truck and a single pair of drivers. The "Sandusky" was bought by the Mad River Railway Company of Ohio, and the gauge of the road was established to suit the engine-- 4 feet 10 inches.

Rogers began by building inside connected engines, but he soon became convinced that outside connected engines were cheaper to build and easier to maintain. That led him gradually into building nothing but outside connected engines. The size of the engine was increased year after year. About 1850 Rogers engines had reached what we consider standard forms, horizontal boiler with wagon top firebox with dome on top; four-wheel coupled drivers about five feet diameter, and four-wheel spread truck which made room for horizontal cylinders about 16x22 inches. Engines of this kind carrying about 120 pounds boiler pressure had about 9,000 pounds tractive power. A ten-wheel engine was built in 1848, and was not unlike a modern engine of that type, except that the cylinders were inclined and a Bury firebox was used.

Hinkley began building locomotives in Boston in 1839, and his first engine, the "Lion," had outside cylinders and two pairs of coupled drivers without a truck. The boiler was straight, and the firebox had a slightly raised wagon top. This style of engine did not satisfy the builder, for he changed to inside cylinders when other builders and railroad companies were abandoning that form. This firm afterwards followed the prevailing fashion of building outside connected engines, but Mr. Hinkley is said to have regretted making the change. By this time all our locomotive builders had adopted the bar frame, and they were doing their best to build engines that were convenient to handle and easy to repair. These have always been peculiarities of American locomotives, and was brought about by most of the railway master mechanics having been locomotive engineers.

New England is reputed to have exerted considerable influence in helping to develope the locomotive on sound lines. Although this section was late in turning to locomotive building, the leaders were masters in the engineering art. Hinkley and Mason and Blood were giants, while there were some master mechanics such as Griggs and Eddy whose work ought to have made them famous. Prominent among these was Wilson Eddy of the Boston & Albany, whose engine, the "Addison Gilmore," Fig. 13, built in 1851, was justly celebrated. The boiler was straight and without a dome. The cylinders, 15-3/8x26 inches, were horizontal, the engine truck wheel being built very low and the wheels spread a little to make room for the cylinders. The driving wheels were single, with a pair of carrying wheels behind, an arrangement that was soon changed for two-pairs of drivers coupled. The frames are made with a splice ahead of the forward pedestal jaw to facilitate repairs. The "Addison Gilmore" had the prototype of the first modern cab. The engine was noted for the shortness of the steam ports, a peculiarity which Mr. Eddy deliberately favored. All his engines were noted for economy in the use of steam.

Everybody is now familiar with the wide fire-box extending over frames, which is generally known as the Wootten type of boiler. In speaking of such engines the real inventor's name is seldom named, for it was not Mr. Wootten, who was merely an improver of the engine. The real inventory was Zerah Colburn, who afterwards started London"Engineering." His engine, shown in Fig. 14, was designed by the New Jersey Locomotive Works, and burned anthracite coal

which it did very successfully. He afterwards designed engines of a similar design which were built for a railroad in Canada and burned bituminous coal.

Early in the fifties locomotive builders had settled down upon what is known as the American locomotive, and succeeding progress for passenger service was mostly devoted to improving details and increasing proportions. The most common engine of this class had cylinders 16x24 inches, drivers 60 inches diameter, and carried about 140 pounds steam pressure. Until about 1880, the eight-wheel engine was used almost entirely for both passenger and freight service, except on mineral and mountain railroads. It gradually increased to the proportions shown in Fig. 15, which has cylinders 20x26 inches, driving wheels 72 inches diameter, a boiler carrying 200 pounds steam pressure, and developing 24,555 pounds tractive power.

Within the last decade, the ordinary locomotive boiler, with fire-box between or raised above the frames, became unequal to the requirements of steam production, and the American engine is giving place to the Atlantic type, Fig. 16, having the driving wheels in front of the firebox and a pair of carrying wheels behind. By this arrangement the fire-box can be made as wide as a sleeping car, if necessary. That has not to be done, of course, but the plan effects a double improvement on the engine. It gives the designer the means of providing a liberal grate area in proportion to the heating surface, and it puts the grate area in a shape in which it can be fired conveniently.

It cannot be denied that the old types of firebox were providing very meagre grate area for the heating surface. For the last ten years, with the powerful passenger engines called for, the ratio of

Fig.13

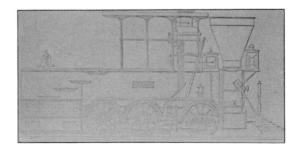

Fig. 14

Fig. 15

Fig. 16

Fig.17

grate area to heating surface has varied from 70 to 80. The passenger engines of twenty-five years ago generally had about fifty square feet of heating surface for each square foot of grate. The wide firebox in the Atlantic type of engines is giving designers the means of providing the grate and heated surface proportions of the old engines. In a number of the most recent Atlantic type engines which I have examined, the ratio of grate to heating surface is about 1 to 50. In some exceptional cases the ratio goes down to about 1 to 70, which is nearly the average of the eight-wheel engine, but in the cases examined the heating surface was abnormally high.

The trend of railroad progress is to move freight with the least possible proportion of dead weight to paying load, and to move it in trains as heavy as can be operated safely. This policy is calling for 50-ton cars and 100-ton locomotives. Fig. 17 shows a decapod tandem compound locomotive, recently built by the American

Locomotive Company in their Schenectady Works for the Atchison, Topeka & Santa Fe, which is the largest locomotive in the world. It weighs 259,800 pounds = 126.9 tons. The cylinders are 17-1/2 and 30 inches by 34-inch stroke, and the driving wheels are 57 inches diameter. The boiler carries 225 pounds of steam to the square inch. Based on these figures the tractive force of the engine is 57,570 pounds, nearly twenty times the power developed by the Gowan & Marx which first made the American locomotive famous as a freight hauler.

A question that we are all very much interested in is the difference in the efficiency of American and of foreign locomotives. You are all more or less familiar with the appearance of foreign engines through the pages of the technical press, if you have not seen them in real steel, iron, and paint. I can show you the outlines of the engines, but I cannot reproduce the colors in which the locomotives belonging to foreign roads are painted.

Fig. 18 shows an outside connected Caledonian engine which was famous in its day. It is in the straight line of development for the popular single-driver engine, the small trailing wheels having been replaced by a pair of drivers.

That engine held its own for many years, but yielded position to the type of eight-wheel inside connected engine shown in Fig. 19, which is one of the heaviest passenger engines in Great Britain and is known as McIntosh's "Bredalbanes."

The "Princess of Wales," Fig. 20, is a Midland Express engine with single drivers. In view of our ten-wheelers and prairie engines for passenger service, we incline to believe that the day of the single-driver engine has departed, but they still hold favor on some British railways. Fig. 21 is an oil burning locomotive belonging to the Great

Fig. 18

Fig. 19

Fig. 21

Fig. 20

Fig. 22

Eastern Railway of England.

The French have put their own personality very strongly upon their railroad rolling stock, and Fig. 22 is a good illustration. That is an express engine designed by Mr. Salmon, chief engineer of the Eastern Railway of France, and is highly efficient for pulling heavy fast trains.

More important than the appearance of the foreign locomotives is their efficiency in service, as compared with American locomotives of similar proportions doing a similar measure of work. A thing that struck me very forcibly the first time I rode upon an American locomotive pulling a passenger train was the heavy consumption of coal. My observation leads me to believe that the American locomotive uses up from ten to twenty-five per cent more fuel than a British engine doing the same measure of work. The evidence of others who have investigated this subject appears to corroborate my views. Now the important question comes up--what is the cause of this difference?

Those to whom I have talked about this on this side of the Atlantic always say that the differences in the fuel. That British locomotives burn much better fuel than ours do. This contention is not well founded. There is no fuel in the world

better than Pocahontas coal, but its use does not bring our locomotives up to the performance of British engines, the majority of which burn coal that possesses about the same heat generating properties as the average Illinois coal. There is no mystery about the properties of fuel, for tables showing analysis of the principal coals in the world are easily procured by any engineering student.

I have devoted considerable attention to identifying the cause of the difference in the economical efficiency of the engines in the two countries, but with very unsatisfactory results. British locomotives as a rule have smaller heating surface than ours, and their proportion of grate area to heating surface is about the same as that found in our locomotives built twenty years ago. The only radical difference between the locomotives is in the steam ports and in the travel of valves. Their steam ports are seldom greater than half the size of ours and the extreme valve travel ranges from 4 to 5 inches. They have no obstruction to draft in the form of spark arrestors which counts for something, but not enough to account for the difference in coal consumption.

I refer the question to the consideration of you and other railroad engineers.

Time Capsule, 1910

The first decade of the present century marked the apogee of the railroads in America. The track system was near its peak and the steam engineering of the trains was in its maturity. In 1910, if you wanted to travel anywhere beyond a few miles from home or ship anything to any distant place, you most likely did so by rail. There was little alternative. Automobiles and trucks were in their infancy and commercial aviation was still the pipe dream of a few wild-eyed airplane enthusiasts. After 1910, however, the steam engines were living on borrowed time and the railroads themselves were rapidly approaching the start of a long decline. Few of them realized it at the time, of course. Epochal changes are often only dimly perceived at the time. So, it is interesting to examine and compare the railroads of 1910:

Atchison, Topeka and
Santa Fe Railroad System

States Served: Illinois, Iowa, Missouri, Kansas, Nebraska, Colorado, Texas, New Mexico, Arizona, California, Oklahoma, Louisiana.

Total earnings for year ending June 30, 1910: $104,993,194.

Total Mileage: Atchison, Topeka and Santa Fe Railroad, 5,563.08 miles; Coast Lines, 1,908.08 miles; Southern Kansas Ry. of Texas, 125.08 miles; Santa Fe, Prescott & Phoenix Ry., 364.24 miles; Eastern Ry. of New Mexico, 433.38 miles; Gulf, Colorado & Santa Fe Ry.1,518.18 miles; Grand Canyon Ry, 66.89 miles. Total mileage, 9,961.25.

Atlantic Coast Line Railroad

States Served: Virginia, North Carolina, South Carolina, Georgia, Florida, Alabama.

Total earnings for year ending June 30,

1909: $26,144,064.

Total Mileage: Virginia, 138.84 miles; North Carolina, 1,022.37 miles; South Carolina, 875,65 miles; Georgia, 714.98 miles; Florida, 1,476.85 miles; Alabama, 247.33 miles. Total mileage, 4,476.02.

Baltimore & Ohio Railroad

States Served: New Jersey, Pennsylvania, Delaware, Maryland, District of Columbia, Virginia, West Virginia, Ohio, Illinois, Indiana, Kentucky, Missouri.

Total earnings for year ending June 30, 1910: $90,163,400.

Total Mileage: Lines included in income account 4,006.32 miles; affiliated lines, 455.78 miles. Total mileage, 4,462.10.

Bangor and Aroostook Railroad

States Served: Maine

Total earnings for year ending June 30, 1910: $2,990,529.

Total Mileage: Brownville to Caribou, 154.95 miles; Oldtown to Greenville, 76 miles; Ashland Junction to Fort Kent, 94.89 miles; Caribou to Van Buren, 33.11 miles; South Lagrange to Searsport, 54.13 miles; Stockholm to Squa Pan, 48.32 miles; Medford Extension (new line), 29.45 miles; Grand Isle to Fort Kent, 30 miles branches and spurs, 116.71 miles. Total mileage, 632.20.

Boston and Albany Railroad

States Served: Massachusetts, New York

Total earnings for year ending: N.A.

Total Mileage: Main Line, Boston, Mass., to Albany, N.Y., 200 miles; Ware River Br., 49 miles; Athol Br., 45 miles; Pittsfield and North

Adams Br, 19 miles; Hudson and Chatham Br, 17 miles; Milford Br., 12 miles; Webster Br., 11 miles; other branches, 39 miles. Total mileage, 392.

Boston and Maine Railroad

States Served: New York, Massachusetts, Vermont, New Hampshire, Maine, Quebec

Total earnings for year ending June 30, 1910: $43,357,175.

Total Mileage: Main Lines (Boston to Portland, via Dover), 115 31 miles; (Boston to Portland via Portsmouth); 108 29 miles; Jewett, Me, to Intervale, N.H., 73 37 miles; Worcester, Mass., to Portland, Me., 148.34 miles; Boston, Mass, to Groveton, N.H., 221.84 miles; Concord, N.H., to White River Jct., Vt., 69.50 miles; White River Jct, Vt. to Lenoxville, P.Q., 142.25 miles; N. Cambridge Jct. to Northampton; Mass., 95.69 miles; Springfield, Mass., to Keene, N.H., 74 miles; Boston to Rotterdam Jct. and Troy, 250.98 miles; Ashburnham Jct. to Bellows Falls, 53.85 miles; branches, 936.91 miles. Total mileage, 2,290.33.

Buffalo, Rochester and Pittsburgh Railway

States Served: New York, Pennsylvania

Total earnings for year ending June 30, 1910: $8,936,116.

Total Mileage: Main Line and branches, 346.39 miles; leased lines, 94.00 miles; trackage rights, 126.66 miles. Total mileage, 567.05

Canadian Northern Railway

States Served: Manitoba, Saskatchewan, Alberta, Ontario, Minnesota

Total earnings for year ending June 30, 1910: $13,833,061.

Total Mileage, 3,297.

Canadian Pacific Railway

States Served: New Brunswick, Maine,Quebec, Ontario, Michigan, Manitoba, Saskatchewan, Alberta, British Columbia.

Total earnings for year ending June 30, 1910: $94,989,490.

Total Mileage: Atlantic Div., 690.2 miles; Eastern Div., 1,364.8 miles; Ontario Div., 1,125.3 miles; Lake Superior Div., 1,102.7 miles Manitoba Div., 2,286.7 miles; Saskatchewan Div., 1,281.4 miles; Alberta Div., 1,436.4 miles; British Columbia Div., 983.1 miles. Total mileage, 10,270.6.

Central of Georgia Railway

States Served: Georgia, Alabama, and Tennessee.

Total earnings for year ending June 30, 1910: $12,052,756.

Total Mileage: Columbus-Andalusia, 138 miles; Griffin-Chattanooga, 198 miles; Macon-Athens, 105 miles; Savannah-Atlanta, 294 miles; Birmingham-Macon, 257 miles; Ft. Valley-Montgomery, 194 miles Smithville-Lockhart, 178 miles; other branches, 551.9 miles. Total mileage, 1.915.9.

Central Railroad of New Jersey

States Served: New York, New Jersey, Pennsylvania

Total earnings for year ending June 30, 1910: $26,586,665.

Total Mileage: New York to Scranton, 191.67 miles; Newark Br., 10.62 miles; South Br., 15.78 miles; Perth Amboy Br., 23.56 miles; High Bridge Br., 55.80 miles; sundry branches in New Jersey , 22.98 miles; sundry branches in Pennsylvania, 108.57 miles; New Jersey Southern Div., 177.90 miles, Freehold and Atlantic Highlands Div., 24.47 miles; New York and Long Branch R.R. 38.04 miles. Total mileage, 669.39.

Central Vermont Railway

States Served: Connecticut, Massachusetts, Vermont, Quebec

Total earnings for year ending June 30, 1910: $4,088,411

Total Mileage: Southern Div., 173.5 miles; Northern Div. 362.6 miles. Total mileage, 537.

Chesapeake & Ohio Railway

States Served: Virginia, West Virginia,

Kentucky, Ohio, Indiana

Total earnings for year ending June 30, 1910: $31,237,169.

Total Mileage: Main Line 664.9 miles; Louisville Line, 208.4 miles; James River Line, 229.9 miles; Washington Line, 94.5 miles; other branches, 766.2 miles; Chesapeake & Ohio Ry. of Indiana. Total mileage, 2,248.4.

Chicago and Alton Railroad

States Served: Illinois and Missouri

Total earnings for year ending June 30, 1910: $13,358,474.

Total Mileage: Chicago to East St. Louis, 279.94 miles; Pequot Line, 26.91 miles; Dwight to Peoria, 81.95 miles; Peoria to Springfield, 55.69 miles; Bloomington to Roodhouse, via Jacksonville, 110.41 miles; Eldred to Barnett Junction, 48.62 miles; Roodhouse to Kansas City, 251.85 miles; Mexico to Cedar City, 50.12 miles, branches, 92.54 miles . Total mileage, 998.09.

Chicago and Eastern Illinois Railroad

States Served: Indiana and Illinois.

Total earnings for year ending June 30, 1910: $11,750,355.

Total Mileage: Merged with the St. Louis & San Francisco Railroad.

Chicago and Northwestern Railway, "The Northwestern Line"

States Served: Michigan, Illinois, Iowa, Wisconsin, Nebraska, Minnesota, North Dakota, South Dakota, Wyoming.

Total earnings for year ending June 30, 1910: $74,175,684.

Total Mileage: Wisconsin Div., 326.93 miles; Galena Div. 497,98 miles; Iowa Div., 569.46 miles; Madison Div., 510 80 miles; Minnesota, 499 88; Dakota Div., 802.68 miles; Peninsula Div., 464.44 miles; Iowa and Minnesota Div., 323.11 miles; Northern Iowa Div., 383 57 miles; Ashland Div., 658.66 miles; Northern Wisconsin Div., 332.72 miles; Sioux City Div., 416.15 miles; Lake Shore Div., 381.35 miles; Nebraska & Wyoming Div., 1,461.66 miles. Total

mileage 7,629.39; Chicago, St. Paul Minn. & O. Ry., 1,729.56

Chicago, Burlington and Quincy Railroad, "The Burlington Route"

States Served: Illinois, Wisconsin, Minnesota, Iowa, Missouri, Nebraska, Kansas, Colorado, Wyoming, South Dakota, Montana.

Total earnings for year ending June 30, 1910: $87,869,517.

Total Mileage: Lines in Illinois, 1,683 miles; in Wisconsin 223.10 miles; in Minnesota, 38.45 miles; in Iowa. 1,439.12 miles; in Missouri 1,392.45 miles; in Nebraska, 2,865.48 miles; in Kansas, 260.14 miles; in Colorado, 429.35 miles; in Montana, 199.90 miles; in South Dakota, 292.01 miles; in Wyoming, 471.29 miles. Total mileage, 9,212.31.

Chicago Great Western Railway

States Served: Illinois, Iowa, Minnesota, Missouri, Kansas, Nebraska.

Total earnings for year ending June 30, 1910: $10,171,783.

Total Mileage: Minneapolis to Chicago, 435.78 miles; Oelwein to Kansas City, 362.34 miles; Hayfield to Clarion, 99.71 miles; Oelwein to Omaha, 267.95 miles; De Kalb Br., 5.81 miles; Cedar Falls Br., 7.48 miles; Mantorville Br., 6.95 miles; Lehigh Br., 15.69 miles; Mankato-Osage Line, 213.90 miles; Winona-Simpson Line, 54.20 miles; other branches, 40.7 miles. Total mileage, 1,510.53.

Chicago, Indianapolis and Louisville Railway

States Served: Indiana, Illinois, Kentucky.

Total earnings for year ending June 30, 1910: $6,020,241.

Total Mileage: Chicago to Louisville, 325.3 miles; Monon to Indianapolis, 95.1 miles: Bloomfield Br. 40.3 miles; Michigan City Div., 60 miles; French Lick Br., 18 miles. Total mileage, 537.9.

Chicago, Milwaukee & Puget Sound Railway

States Served: South Dakota, North Dakota, Montana, Idaho, Washington.

Total earnings for year ending June 30, 1910: $10,765,703.

Total Mileage: Mobridge, S.Dak., to Tacoma, Wash., 1,411 miles; Lewiston Br., 63 miles; Elk River Br., 72 miles; Hoquiam Br., 95 miles; Moreau River Line, 55 miles; New England Br., 134 miles; Takoma Eastern R.R., 73 miles. Total mileage, 1,903.

Chicago, Milwaukee and St. Paul Railway

States Served: Illinois, Wisconsin, Michigan, Minnesota, Iowa, Missouri, South Dakota, North Dakota

Total earnings for year ending June 30, 1910: $64,846,893

Total Mileage: Lines in Illinois, 414.99 miles; in Wisconsin, 1,783.10 miles; in Iowa, 1,871.09 miles; in Minnesota, 1,241.05 miles; in North Dakota, 153.31 miles; in South Dakota, 1,529.66 miles; in Missouri, 140.27 miles; in Michigan, 159.12 miles. Total mileage, 7,296.55.

Chicago, Rock Island and Pacific Railway

States Served: Illinois, Iowa, Minnesota, South Dakota, Missouri, Nebraska, Kansas, Oklahoma, Colorado, Tennessee, Arkansas, Louisiana.

Total earnings for year ending August 31, 1910: $62,348,510.

Total Mileage: Chicago-Colorado Springs, 1,070.05 miles: Davenport-Terral, 829.94 miles; Herington-Texhoma, 323.33 miles; Keokuk-Des Moines, 162 40 miles; DesMoines-Sibley, 176.35 miles; Burlington-Minneapolis, 365.62 miles; Vinton-Watertown, 375.97 miles; Memphis-Texola, 649.40 miles; Haskell-Eunice, 302.80 miles; Kansas City-St. Louis, 298.50 miles; other lines and branches, 2,841.35 miles. Total mileage, 7,395.71.

Cincinnati, Hamilton & Dayton Ry.

States Served: Ohio, Indiana, Illinois.

Total earnings for year ending: N.A.

Total Mileage: Main line and branches, 1,037.80 miles.

Cleveland, Cincinnati, Chicago & St. Louis Railway

States Served: Ohio, Indiana, Michigan, Illinois.

Total earnings for year ending December 31, 1909: $27,963,065.

Total Mileage: Cleveland-Indianapolis Div., 341 miles; Mt. Gilead Short Line, 2 miles; Cincinnati-Sandusky Div., 369 miles; St. Louis Div., 309 miles; Chicago Div., 321 miles; Cairo Div., 270 miles; Peoria and Eastern Div., 352 miles; White Water Div., 70 miles; Michigan Div., 302 miles; Kankakee and Seneca Div., 42 miles. Total mileage, 2,378.

Colorado and Southern Railway, "The Colorado Road"

States Served: Colorado, Wyoming, New Mexico.

Total earnings for year ending June 30, 1910: $16,777,980.

Total Mileage: Pueblo Dist., 134.05 miles; Trinidad Dist.,115.33 miles; New Mexico Dist., 150.13 miles; Clear Creek Dist., 66.10 miles; Ft. Collins Dist., 178.01 miles; Platte Canon Dist., 106.12 miles; Leadville Dist., 74.36 miles; Gunnison Dist., 163.64 miles; Wyoming Dist. 260.03 miles. Total mileage 1,247.86. Fort Worth and Denver City Ry., 454.14 miles. Total mileag, 2,949.77.

Colorado Midland Railway

States Served: Colorado

Total earnings for year ending June 30, 1910: $2,340,285.

Total Mileage: Colorado Springs, Col., to Grand Junction, Col., 302 miles; Aspen Br., 18 miles; Jerome Park Br., 15 miles. Total mileage, 335.

Delaware and Hudson Railroad

States Served: Pennsylvania, New York, Vermont

Total earnings for year ending June 30, 1910: $19,868,799.

Total Mileage: Pennsylvania Div., 128.29 miles; Saratoga Div., 251.14 miles; Champlain Div., 230.69 miles; Susquehanna Div., 233.34 miles. Total mileage, 843.46.

Delaware, Lackawanna and Western Railroad

States Served: New York, New Jersey, Pennsylvania.

Total earnings for year ending June 30, 1910: $36,005,987.

Total Mileage: Main Line, Hoboken, N.J. to Buffalo, N.Y., 409.33 miles; Morristown Line., 34.46 miles; Sussex R.R. 30.55 miles; Bangor and Portland Br., 38.38 miles; Bloomsburg Br., 79.64 miles; S.B. & N.Y. R.R., 80.95 miles; Oswego & Syracuse Div., 34.98 miles; Utica Div., 105.51 miles; Ithaca Br., 34.41 miles; Lackawanna & Montrose R.R., 10.48 miles; other branches, 98.07 miles. Total mileage, 956.76.

Denver and Rio Grande Railroad

States Served: Colorado, Utah and New Mexico.

Total earnings for year ending June 30, 1910: $23,563,436.

Total Mileage: Denver to Ogden, 778 miles; Salida to Grand Junction, via Gunnison, 208.92 miles; Cuchara Junction to Silverton, 328.47 miles; Antonito to Santa Fe, 125.79 miles; Pueblo to Trinidad, 91.55 miles; Carbon Junction to Farmington, 47.66 miles; Marysvale Branch, 132.51 miles; Tintic Branch, 43.75 miles; Provo Canon Branch, 26 miles; Park City Branch, 32.28 miles; San Pete Valley Branch 34.63 miles; Morrison Branch, 15.05 miles; other branches, 733.12. Total mileage, 2,597.73.

Detroit and Mackinac Railway

States Served: Michigan

Total earnings for year ending June 30,

1910: $1,231,243.

Total Mileage: Bay City to Cheboygan, 196.24 miles; Prescott Div., 11.85 miles; Rose City Div., 31.21 miles; Lincoln Br., 14.4 miles Au Gres Br., 7.95 miles; Hillman Br., 22.40 miles; logging branches, 80.4 miles. Total mileage, 364.49.

Detroit, Toledo and Ironton Railway

States Served: Michigan and Ohio.

Total earnings for year ending June 30, 1910: $1,607,031.

Total Mileage: Detroit, Toledo & Ironton Ry., 436 miles.

Duluth, South Shore and Atlantic Ry.

States Served: Michigan, Wisconsin, Minnesota

Total earnings for year ending June 30, 1910: $3,302,147.

Total Mileage: Main Line, 517.44 miles; other branches, 67.54 miles. Total mileage, 584.98.

El Paso & Southwestern System

States Served: Texas, New Mexico, Arizona

Total earnings for year ending June 30, 1909: $7,274.014.

Total Mileage: Western Div., 383.8 miles; Eastern Div., 518.8 miles. Total mileage, 902.6.

Erie Railroad

States Served: New York, New Jersey, Pennsylvania, Ohio, Indiana, Illinois.

Total earnings for year ending June 30, 1910: $51,830,720.

Total Mileage: New York Div., 234.87 miles; Northern R.R., 26.05 miles; Greenwood Lake, 53.30 miles; Delaware Div., 104.40 miles, Wyoming Div., 82.84 miles; Jefferson Div., 43.34 miles; Susquehanna Div., 139.70 miles; Tioga Division, 4.68 miles Rochester Div., 144.37 miles; Buffalo Div., 188.17 miles; Allegheny Div., 129.48 miles; Bradford div., 88.61 miles; Meadville Div., 238.18 miles; Mahoning Div., 164.05 miles; Cincinnati Div., 197.39 miles; Lima

Div., 126.60 miles; Chicago Div., 122.97 miles; trackage rights, 182.17 miles. Total mileage, 2,331.17.

Florida East Coast Railway
States Served: Florida

Total earnings for year ending June 30, 1909: $3,373,554.

Total Mileage: Jacksonville to Knights Key, 478 miles; branch lines, 98 miles. Total mileage, 576.

Georgia Railroad
States Served: Georgia

Total earnings for year ending June 30, 1909: $2,750,872.

Total Mileage: Augusta, Ga., to Atlanta, Ga. 171 miles; Macon Br., 78 miles; Athens Br., 40 miles; Washington Br., 18 miles. Total mileage, 307.

Georgia Southern and Florida Railway
States Served: Georgia and Florida.

Total earnings for year ending June 30, 1910: $2,322,157.

total Mileage: Macon, Ga., to Palatka, Fla., 285 miles; Valdosta, Ga., to Grand Crossing, Fla., 106.61 miles. Total mileage, 391.61.

Grand Rapids and Indiana Railway
States Served: Indiana and Michigan.

Total earnings for year ending December 31, 1909: $4,861,452.

Total Mileage: Richmond, Ind., to Mackinaw City, Mich., 460 miles; Traverse City Div., 26 miles; Muskegon Div., 36.85 miles; Harbor Springs Br., 5.91 miles; Missaukee, Br., 31.94 miles; other branches, 27.16 miles. Total mileage 587.52.

Grand Trunk Railway
States Served: Maine, New Hampshire, Vermont, Quebec, Ontario, Illinois, Indiana, Michigan

Total earnings for year ending December 31, 1909: $3,632,902

Total Mileage: Eastern Div., 938 miles; Ottawa Div., 466 miles; Middle Div., 1,491 miles; Northern Div., 889 miles; Western Div., 972 miles. Total mileage 4,756.

Great Northern Railway
States Served: Minnesota, North Dakota, South Dakota, Iowa, Nebraska, Montana, Idaho, Washington, Wisconsin.

Total earnings for year ending June 30, 1910: $64,465,369.

Total Mileage: Great Northern Ry. Total mileage, 7,274.38.

Hocking Valley Railway
States Served: Ohio

Total earnings for year ending June 30, 1910: $7,569,330.

Total Mileage: Toledo, O., to Athens, O., 204.5 miles; River Div. (Logan to Pomeroy), 83 miles; Jackson Br. 17.5 miles other branches, 45 miles. Total mileage, 350.

Houston and Texas Central Railroad
States Served: Texas

Total earnings for year ending: N.A. (Financial report included in listing for Southern Pacific Co.)

Total Mileage: Main Line, 337.98 miles; Western Br., 115 miles; Waco Br., 54.77 miles; Austin Div., 129.45 miles; Ft. Worth Br., 52.83 miles; Lancaster Br., 4.75 miles Nelleva-Mexia Cut-off. 94 miles. Total mileage, 788.78.

Illinois Central Railroad
States Served: Illinois, Indiana, Wisconsin, Iowa, Minnesota, South Dakota, Kentucky, Tennessee, Mississippi, Louisiana, Missouri, Alabama, Arkansas.

Total earnings for year ending June 30, 1910: $57,884,721.

Total Mileage: Illinois Central R.R., 2,102.10 miles; Chicago, St. Louis and New Orleans R.R., 1,256.32 miles; Dubuque and Sioux City R.R., 767.88 miles; other branches, 424.24 miles. Total mileage, 4,550.54.

Intercolonial Railway

States Served: Nova Scotia, New Brunswick, Quebec.

Total Earnings for year ending June 30, 1910: $9,268,234.

Total Mileage: Halifax and Montreal Line, 833.67 miles; St. John Br., 89.31 miles; Truro and Sydney Line, 214.27 miles; Oxford and Picton Br., 69.39 miles; Canada Eastern Br., 124.80 miles; other branches, 121.52 miles. Total mileage, 1,452.96.

International and
Great Northern Railroad

States Served: Texas

Total Earnings for year ending June 30, 1909: $8,097,939.

Total Mileage: Gulf Div., 408.9 miles; Fort Worth Div., 372.7 miles; San Antonio Div., 422.9 miles. Total mileage, 1,159.5.

Iowa Central Railway

States Served: Iowa and Illinois.

Total Earnings for year ending June 30, 1909. $3,015,646.

Total Mileage: Albia, Ia., to Albert Lea, Minn., 295.32 miles; Oskaloosa, Ia., to Peoria, Ill. 188.90 miles; other branches, 164.21 miles. Total mileage, 558.43.

Kansas City Southern Railway

Texarkana and Fort Smith Railway.

States Served: Missouri, Kansas, Arkansas, Oklahoma, Louisiana, Texas.

Total Earnings for year ending June 30, 1910: $9,594,651.

Total Mileage: Kansas City, Mo., to Port Arthur, Tex., 788 miles; Fort Smith Br., 16 miles; Lake Charles Br., 23 miles; Air Line Branch, 6 miles. Total mileage, 839.

Lake Erie and Western Railroad

States Served: Ohio, Indiana, Illinois.

Total Earnings for year ending December 31, 1909: $5,043,989.

Total Mileage: Main Line, 415.5 miles;

Indianapolis and Michigan City Div., 159.4 miles; Fort Wayne and Connorsville Div., 108.5 miles; Rushville Br., 24 miles; Minster Br., 9.8 miles; Northern Ohio Ry., 161.7 miles. Total mileage, 878.9.

Lake Shore and
Michigan Southern Railway

States Served: New York, Pennsylvania, Ohio, Michigan, Indiana, Illinois.

Total Earnings for year ending December 31, 1909: $45,533,396.

Total Mileage: Eastern Div., 171 miles; Toledo Div., 194 miles; Michigan Div., 408 miles; Western Div., 112 miles; Franklin Div., 245 miles; Detroit Div., 155 miles; Lansing Div., 290 miles. Total mileage, 1,575.

Lehigh Valley Railroad

States Served: New York, New Jersey, Pennsylvania.

Total Earnings for year ending June 30, 1910: $36,167,398.

Total Mileage: New Jersey and Lehigh Div., 224.63 miles; Mahanoy and Hazleton Div., 193.74 miles; Wyoming Div., 311.36 miles; New York Div., 22.02 miles; Auburn Div., 302.30 miles; Buffalo Div., 331.94 miles. Total mileage, 1,385.99.

Long Island Railroad

States Served: Long Island, New York.

Total Earnings for year ending December 31,1909: $10,898,371.

Total Mileage: Main Line-Long Island City to Greenport, 94.74 miles; Long Island City to Montauk, 115.13 miles; branches owned, 106.48 miles; branches leased, 63.75 miles; New York and Rockaway Beach Ry., 11.74 miles. Total mileage, 391.84.

Louisville and Nashville Railroad

States Served: Kentucky, Indiana, Illinois, Georgia, North Carolina, Virginia, Tennessee, Alabama, Florida, Louisiana, Mississippi.

Total Earnings for year ending June 30,

1910: $52,433,381.

Total Mileage: Cincinnati to Louisville, 114 miles; Louisville to Nashville, 187 miles; Nashville to New Orleans, 622 miles; Memphis Junction to Memphis, 260 miles; E. St. Louis to Edgefield Junction, 310 miles; Louisville to Lexington, 94 miles; Cincinnati to Atlanta, 485 miles; other branches, 2,326.37 miles. Total mileage, 4,398.37.

Main Central Railroad

States Served: Maine, New Hampshire, Vermont, Quebec.

Total Earnings for year ending June 30, 1910: $8,922,312.

Total Mileage: Portland to Vanceboro, via Augusta, 250.88 miles; Cumberland Junction to Skowhegan, 91.20 miles; Bath to Lewiston and Farmington, 76.30 miles; Belfast Br., 33.13 miles; Dexter Br.,30.77 miles; Brewer Junction to Mt. Desert Ferry, 41.13 miles; Portland to Lunenburg, 109.10 miles; Quebec Junction to Lime Ridge, 108.18 miles; Woolwich to Rockland, 47.13 miles; branches and industrial tracks, 144.12 miles. Total mileage, 931.94.

Michigan Central Railroad

States Served: New York, Ontario, Michigan, Ohio, Indiana, Illinois

Total Earnings for year ending December 31, 1909: $27,905,394.

Total Mileage: Main Line, Buffalo to Chicago, 535.9 miles; Toledo Div., 59.9 miles; St. Clair Div., 66.4 miles; Grand Rapids Div., 94.4 miles; Mackinaw Div., 182.3 miles; Air Line Div., 104.3 miles; Saginaw Div., 115.3 miles; Bay City Div., 108.9 miles; Saginaw Bay and N.W. Div., 27.4 miles; other branches, 482.3 miles. Total mileage, 1,776.20.

Minneapolis & St. Louis Railroad, "The Albert Lea Route"

States Served: Minnesota, Iowa, S.Dakota.

Total Earnings for year ending June 30, 1909: $4,171,315.

Total Mileage: St. Paul, Albert Lea and Southern Divs., 271.15 miles; Western and Pacific Div., 216.07 miles; Southwestern Div., 153.50 miles; Des Moines & Ft. Dodge Div., 156.72 miles; M.D. & P. Div., 229.60 miles. Total mileage, 1,027.04.

Minneapolis, St. Paul and Sault Ste. Marie Railway, "The Soo Line"

States Served: Illinois, Michigan, Wisconsin, Minnesota, North Dakota, South Dakota.

Total Earnings for year ending: June 30, 1910: $15,407,179.

Total Mileage: East of Minneapolis, 632.15 miles; west of St. Paul, 1,835.27 miles; Chicago Division (Wisconsin Central) 1,056.91 miles. Total mileage, 3,533.06.

Missouri, Kansas and Texas Railway

States Served: Missouri, Kansas, Oklahoma, Texas, Louisiana.

Total Earnings for year ending June 30, 1910: $26,559,346.

Total Mileage: Missouri, Kansas & Texas Ry., 1,725 miles; Missouri, Kansas & Texas Ry. of Texas, 1,245 miles; Galveston, Houston & Henderson R.R. 50 miles, Denison, Bonham & New Orleans R.R., 24 miles; Wichita Falls Ry., 18 miles; Dallas, Cleburne & Southwestern R.R., 10 miles. Total mileage, 3,072.

Missouri Pacific System

States Served: Missouri, Kansas, Nebraska, Colorado, Oklahoma, Arkansas, Louisiana, Tennessee, Illinois.

Total Earnings for year ending June 30, 1908: $44,238,702.

Total Mileage: Missouri Pacific Ry., 3,883.43 miles; St. Louis, Iron Mountain and Southern Ry., 3,287.84 miles. Total mileage, 7,171.27.

Mobile and Ohio Railroad

States Served: Missouri, Illinois, Kentucky, Tennessee, Mississippi, Alabama.

Total Earnings for year ending June 30, 1910: $10,636,732.

Total Mileage: Main Line, St. Louis, Mo., to Mobile, Ala., 644.83 miles; Aberdeen Br., 9 miles; Starkville Br., 11 miles; Montgomery Div., 167.18 miles; Blocton Br., 12.90 miles; Columbus, Miss. Br., 14 miles; Warrior Southern R.R., 13.60 miles; Warrior Br., 9.51 miles; Millstadt Br., 7 miles; Mobile and Bay Shore Ry., 38.36 miles. Total mileage, 927.38.

Nashville, Chattanooga and St. Louis Railway, "Lookout Mountain Route"

States Served: Georgia, Alabama, Tennessee , Kentucky.

Total Earnings for year ending June 30, 1910: $11,637,203.

Total Mileage: Main Line, 320.21 miles; McMinnville Br., 84.60 miles; Sequatchie Valley Br., 68.10 miles; Tracy City Br., 31.17 miles; Centreville Br., 69.91 miles; Shelbyville Br., 8.01 miles; Lebanon Br., 29.21 miles; Western and Atlantic R.R., 136.82 miles; Rome R.R., 18.15 miles; Huntsville and Gadsden Br., 80.08 miles; Fayetteville and Columbia Br., 86.35 miles; Paducah and Memphis Div., 254.20 miles; Middle Tenn. and Ala. Br., 36.98 miles; West Nashville Br., 6.26 miles. Total mileage, 1,230.05.

New Orleans, Mobile and Chicago Railroad

States Served: Alabama, Mississippi, Tennessee.

Total Earnings for year ending: N.A.

Total Mileage: Main Line, 366.5 miles; Hattiesburg Br., 26.9 miles. Total mileage, 393.4.

New York Central and Hudson River Railroad

States Served: New York, New Jersey, Pennsylvania, Massachusetts.

Total Earnings for year ending December 31, 1909: $97,689,857.

Total Mileage: New York Central and Hudson River R.R., 805.47 miles; West Shore R.R., 478.94 miles; New York and Harlem R.R., 136.48 miles; Rome, Watertown and Ogdensburg R.R., 624.15 miles; Beech Creek R.R., 164.67 miles; Beech Creek Extension R.R., 127.50 miles; Mohawk and Malone Ry., 182.18 miles; Carthage and Adirondack Ry., 45.86 miles; New York and Putnam R.R., 58.88 miles; Geneva, Corning & Southern R.R., 231.71 miles; Wallkil Valley R.R., 32.88 miles; other roads, 44.04 miles; New York & Ottawa Line 128.40 miles; St. Lawrence and Adirondack Ry., 65.29 miles. Lines operated under trackage rights, 261.67 miles; Boston & Albany R.R., 392.65 miles. Total mileage, 3,781.83.

New York, Chicago and St. Louis Railroad

States Served: New York, Pennsylvania, Ohio, Indiana, Illinois

Total Earnings for year ending June 30, 1910: $10,854,256.

Total Mileage: Buffalo, N.Y. to Chicago, Ill. 523 miles;

New York, New Haven & Hartford Railroad

States Served: Massachusetts, Rhode Island, Connecticut, New York.

Total Earnings for year ending June 30, 1910: $64,256,416.

Total Mileage: New York Div., 41.90 miles; Shore Line Div., 390.79 miles; Providence Div., 316.52 miles; Boston Div., 84.15 miles; Midland Div., 350.40 miles; Old Colony Div., 462.96 miles; Western Div., 353.32 miles. Total mileage , 2,000.04.

New York, Ontario and Western Railway

States Served: New York, Pennsylvania

Total Earnings for year ending June 30, 1910: $8,578,782.

Total Mileage: Main Line, Cornwall, N.Y., to Oswego, N.Y., 271.75 miles; Delhi Br., 16.84 miles; Wharton Valley R.R., 6.80 miles; New Berlin Br., 22.38 miles; Utica Div., 31.30 miles; Rome Br., 12.78 miles; Scranton Div., 54.05 miles; Ellenville Br., 7.80 miles; Pecksport Ry., 3.69 miles; Weehawken, N.J., to Cornwall, N.Y. (trackage rights), 53.07 miles; Ellenville and

Kingston R.R., 27.14 miles; Port Jervis, Mont. and Sum. R.R., 38.27 miles. Total mileage, 545.87.

New York, Susquehanna & Western Railroad

 States Served: New Jersey, New York and Pennsylvania

 Total Earnings for year ending June 30, 1909: $3,252,745.

 Total Mileage: Main Line, Jersey City, N.J., to Stroudsburg, Pa., 126.23 miles; Wilkes-Barre and Eastern R.R., 72.86 miles; Middletown Div., 34.15 miles. Total mileage, 233.24.

Norfolk Southern Railroad

 States Served: Virginia, North Carolina

 Total Earnings for year ending: N.A.

 Total Mileage: Main Line and branches, 592 miles.

Norfolk and Western Railway

 States Served: Maryland, West Virginia, Virginia, North Caroline, Ohio, Kentucky.

 Total Earnings for year ending June 30, 1910: $35,063,870.

 Total Mileage: Norfolk to Columbus, O., 703.76 miles; Lynchburg to Durham, 115.43 miles; Roanoke to Hagerstown, 238.11 miles; Roanoke to Winston-Salem, 121.30 miles; Radford Junction to Bristol, 110.75 miles; North Carolina Junction to Fries, 43.49 miles; Graham to Norton, 100.40 miles; Portsmouth Junction to Cincinnati and Ivorydale, 105.92 miles; Columbus, Connecting and Terminal R.R., 3.51 miles; branches, 394.63 miles. Total mileage, 1,937.30.

Northern Pacific Railway, "The Yellowstone Park Line"

 States Served: Wisconsin, Minnesota, North Dakota, Montana, Idaho, Washington, Oregon.

 Total Earnings for year ending June 30, 1910: $74,525,826.

 Total Mileage: St. Paul, Minn., to Portland, Ore., Tacoma and Seattle, Wash., 2,837.77 miles; other divisions and branches, 2,976.35 miles. Total

mileage, 5,814.12.

Northwestern Pacific Railroad

 States Served: California

 Total Earnings for year ending June 30, 1910: $3,167.805.

 Total Mileage: San Francisco to Sherwood, Cal., 152 miles; Cazadero Line, 84 miles; Guerneville Br., 28 miles; branches, 144 miles. Total mileage, 408.

Oregon Railroad and Navigation Co.

 States Served: Oregon, Washington, Idaho.

 Total Earnings for year ending: N.A.

 Total Mileage: Portland, Ore., to Huntington, Ore., 405 miles; Spokane Div., 294 miles; other branches, 792 miles. Total mileage, 1,491.

Oregon Short Line Railroad

 States Served: Utah, Wyoming, Idaho, Montana, Oregon.

 Total Earnings for year ending: N.A.

 Total Mileage: Lines in Utah, 208.18 miles; in Wyoming, 123.13 miles; in Idaho, 1,032.80 miles; in Montana, 144.35 miles; in Oregon, 87.66 miles. Total mileage, 1,596.12

Pennsylvania Railroad

 New York, New Jersey, Pennsylvania, Delaware, Maryland, District of Columbia, Virginia, West Virginia, Michigan, Kentucky, Ohio, Indiana, Illinois.

 Total Earnings for year ending December 31, 1909: $315,406,804.

 Total Mileage: Eastern Pennsylvania Div., 1,228.22 miles; Western Pennsylvania Div., 694.19 miles; Philadelphia Terminal Div., 48.72 miles; New Jersey Div., 449.23 miles; Erie Div., 605.03 miles; Northern Central Ry. Div., 460.85 miles; Philadelphia, Baltimore and Washington R.R. Div., 696.88 miles; West Jersey and Sea Shore R.R. Div., 336.72 miles; Buffalo and Allegheny Valley Div., 781.95 miles; Baltimore, Chesapeake and Atlantic Ry., 87.66 miles; Barnegat R.R., 8.15 miles; Cherry Tree and Dixonville R.R.,

37.60 miles; Cumberland Valley R.R. lines, 162.19 miles; Long Island R.R. lines, 390.56 miles; Maryland, Delaware & Virginia Ry., 78.33 miles; Monongahela R.R. lines, 64.93 miles; Pemberton & Heightstown R.R., 24.37 miles; Philadelphia & Beach Haven R.R., 12.80 miles; New York, Philadelphia & Norfolk R.R., 112 miles; other branches, 13.94 miles. Total mileage lines east, 6,294.32. Pennsylvania lines west of Pittsburgh, 4,940.04 miles.

Pere Marquette Railroad

States Served: Michigan, Ohio, Indiana, Illinois, Ontario, Canada

Total earnings for year ending June 30, 1910: $16,542,271.

Total Mileage: Grand Rapids Dist., 770.60 miles; Saginaw Dist. 1,017.29 miles; Detroit Dist., 188.34 miles; lines in Canada (Buffalo Division), 359.67 miles. Total mileage, 2,335.90.

Philadelphia and Reading Railway

States Served: New Jersey, Pennsylvania, Delaware

Total earnings for year ending June 30, 1910: $44,214,914.

Total Mileage: Reading Div., 395.37 miles; Philadelphia Div., 49.01 miles; New York Div., 155.14 miles; Harrisburg Div., 103.62 miles; Shamokin Div., 267.58 miles; Wilmington and Columbia Div., 121.49 miles; other lines operated separately, 490.27 miles. Total mileage, 1,582.48.

Queen and Crescent Route

States Served: Ohio, Kentucky, Tennessee, Georgia, Alabama, Mississippi, Louisiana.

Total earnings for year ending June 30, 1910: $9,079,471.

Total Mileage: Comprising the following lines: Cincinnati, New Orleans and Texas Pacific Ry., 338 miles; New Orleans and Northeastern R.R., 196 miles; Alabama and Vicksburg Ry., 142 miles; Vicksburg, Shreveport and Pacific Ry., 171 miles; Alabama Great southern R.R., 309.41 miles. Total mileage, 1,156.41.

Rutland Railroad

States Served: Vermont and New York

Total earnings for year ending December 31, 1909: $3,102,432.

Total Mileage: White Creek, Vt., to Canada Line, Que., 161.42 miles; Chatham, N.Y. to Bennington, Vt., 57.21 miles;Bennington, Vt., to No. Bennington, 4.67 miles; Bellows Falls, Vt., to Rutland, Vt., 52.21 miles; Alburgh; Vt., to Ogdensburg, N.Y., 121.60 miles; Canada Line to Noyan Jct., Que., 3.39 miles; Leicester Jct., Vt., to Addison Jct., N.Y., 14.61 miles. Total mileage, 415.11.

San Antonio and Aransas Pass Railway

States Served: Texas

Total earnings for year ending June 30, 1909: $3,936,286.

Total Mileage: Houston, Tex., to San Antonio, Tex., 238 miles; Kenedy, Tex., to Corpus Christi, Tex., 88 miles; Rockport Br., 21 miles; Lockhart Br., 55 miles; Alice Br., 43 miles; Waco Br., 171 miles; Kerrville Br., 71 miles; Falfurrias Br., 36.3 miles. Total mileage, 723.7.

San Pedro, Los Angeles and Salt Lake Railroad

States Served: Utah, Nevada, California.

Total earnings for year ending June 30, 1910: $6,092,822.

Total Mileage: Salt Lake City, Utah, to Los Angeles, Cal., 781.2 miles; branches, 290.6 miles. Total mileage, 1,071.8.

Seaboard Air Line Railway

States Served: Virginia, North Carolina, South Carolina, Georgia, Florida, Alabama

Total earnings for year ending June 30, 1910: $20,068,771.

Total Mileage: First Div., 370.35 miles; Second Div., 386.51 miles; Third Div., 398.26 miles; Fourth Div., 534.24 miles; Fifth Div., 462.44 miles; Sixth Div., 459.17 miles; branches, 384.3 miles. Total mileage, 2,995.

Southern Pacific Company, "Sunset, Ogden and Shasta Routes."

States Served: Louisiana, Texas, New Mexico, Arizona, California Nevada, Oregon, Utah.

Total earnings for year ending June 30, 1910: $135,022,606.

Total Mileage:

Lines south of Portland and west of Ogden and Rio Grande: Nevada and California Ry., 443.96 miles; Central Pacific Ry., 1,522.24 miles; Oregon & California R.R., 684.85 miles; South Pacific Coast Ry., 97.13 miles' Southern Pacific R.R., 3,368.59 miles; New Mexico and Arizona R.R. 88.19 miles; Sonora R.R., 263.45 miles. Total mileage, 6,468.41.

Sunset Central Lines: Morgan's Louisiana and Texas R.R. and Steamship Co., 358.51 miles; Iberia and Vermilion R.R., 21.00 miles; Louisiana Western R.R., 198.28 miles; Texas and New Orleans R.R., 458.01 m,iles; Galveston, Harrisburg and San Antonio Ry., 1,338.56 miles; Houston and Texas Central R.R., 789.01 miles; Houston, E. and W. Texas Ry., 190.94 miles; Houston and Shreveport R.R., 39.78 miles. Total mileage 3,393.81.

Southern Railway

States Served: District of Columbia, Virginia, North Carolina, South Carolina, Georgia, Florida, Alabama, Mississippi, Tennessee, Kentucky, Illinois, Indiana, Missouri.

Total earnings for year ending June 30, 1910: $57,294,508.

Total Mileage:

Northern District: Washington Div., 346.23 miles; Danville Div., 371.98 miles Richmond Div., 279.15 miles; Norfolk Div., 427.18 miles; Winston-Salem Div., 380.40 miles. Total, 1,804.94 miles.

Middle District: Knoxville Div., 359.02 miles; Murphy Div., 122.50 miles; Coster Div., 212.18 miles; Memphis Div., 332.13 miles; Asheville Div., 206.90 miles; Carolina & Tennessee, Southern, 13.90 miles; Transylvania Div., 42.10 miles; K.&A., and K.&B., 65.81 miles; Tennessee & Carolina Southern 25.30 miles. Total, 1,379.84 miles.

Eastern District: Charlotte Div., 461.64 miles; Columbia Div., 789.51 miles; Charleston Div., 446.57 miles. Total, 1,697.72 miles.

Western District : Birmingham Div., 349.20 miles; Mobile Div., 569.06 miles; Atlanta Div., 503.71 miles; Columbus Div., 200.28 miles. Total, 1,622.25 miles. St. Louis-Louisville Line, 545.42 miles.

Total mileage of system, 7,050.17.

Spokane, Portland and Seattle Railway

States Served: Washington, Oregon.

Total earnings for year ending: N.A.

Total Mileage: Spokane, Wash., to Portland, Ore.,377.5 miles; Astoria and Columbia River R.R., 119.1 miles; branches, 45.4 miles. Total mileage, 542.

St. Louis Southwestern Railway System, "The Cotton Belt Route."

States Served: Illinois, Missouri, Arkansas, Louisiana, Texas.

Total earnings for year ending June 30, 1910: $10,986,515.

Total Mileage:

St. Louis Southwestern Ry.: Main Line, 428.9 miles; Stuttgart Br., 35.1 miles; New Madrid Br., 6.1 miles; Little Rock Br., 44.4 miles; Shreveport Br., 62.6 miles; Cairo Br., 57.7 miles, Illinois Div. (joint track), 138.2 miles. Total mileage, 773.

St. Louis Southwestern Ry. of Texas: Main Line, 305.4 miles; Sherman Br., 52.3 miles; Fort Worth Br., 154.3 miles; Hillsboro Br., 40.2 miles; Lufkin Br., 130.9 miles; Dallas Br., 13.7 miles. Total mileage, 696.8.

Grand total mileage, 1,469.8.

St. Louis and San Francisco Railroad

States Served: Illinois, Indiana, Missouri, Kansas, Arkansas, Oklahoma, Texas, Tennessee, Mississippi, Alabama.

Total earnings for year ending June 30, 1910: $41,165,939.

Total Mileage: St. Louis & San Francisco R.R. 4,737 miles; Fort Worth & Rio Grande Ry., 195.88 miles; Chicago & Eastern Illinois R.R., 965.68 miles; St. Louis, San Francisco & Texas Ry., 135.64 miles; Paris & Great Northern R.R., 16.94 miles. Total mileage, 6,219.17.

Texas and Pacific Railway

States Served: Louisiana, Arkansas and Texas.

Total earnings for year ending December 31, 1909: $14,960.652.

Total Mileage: Eastern Div., 511 miles; Rio Grande Div., 620 miles; Louisiana Div., 356 miles; Port Allen Br., 102 miles; La Fourche Br., 28 miles; Texarkana Dist., 70 miles; Avoyelles Br., 93 miles; Natchitoches Br., 89 miles; Napoleonville Br., 16 miles. Total mileage, 1,885.

Toledo and Ohio Central Railway, "The New York Central Lines"

States Served: Ohio and West Virginia.

Total earnings for year ending June 30, 1910: $4,476,950.

Total Mileage: Toledo to Bremen, 172.91 miles; New Lexington to Corning, 12.33 miles; Whitmore to Thurston, 145.57 miles; Alum Creek to Truro Junction, 4.20 miles; Peoria to St. Marys, 59.90 miles. Total mileage 394.91.

Toledo, St. Louis and Western Railroad, "The Clover Leaf-Route"

States Served: Ohio, Indiana, Illinois, Missouri.

Total earnings for year endin: June 30, 1910: $3,772,636.

Total Mileage: Toledo, O., to St. Louis, Mo., 450.72 miles.

Union Pacific Railroad, "The Overland Route"

States Served: Kansas, Nebraska, Iowa, Colorado, Wyoming, Utah, Missouri.

Total Mileage: Nebraska Div., 799.54 miles; Kansas Div., 936.45 miles; Colorado Div., 810.29 miles; Wyoming Div., 513.81 miles; Utah

Div., 350.93 miles. Total mileage, 3,411.02.

Vandalia Railroad Company

States Served: Indiana, Illinois

Total earnings for year ending December 31, 1909: $8,387,052.

Total Mileage: St. Louis Div., 242 miles; Centre Point Br., 8 miles; Michigan Div., 275 miles; Vincennes Div., 117 miles; branches, 16 miles; Terre Haute and Peoria R.R., 174 miles. Total mileage, 832.

Virginian Railway

States Served: Virginia, West Virginia.

Total earnings for yeard ending: N.A.

Total mileage: Norfolk, Va., to Deepwater, W.Va. 436 miles; Winding Gulf, Br., 27 miles. Total mileage, 463.

Wabash Railroad

States Served: Ontario, Canada, Ohio, Indiana, Michigan, Illinois, Missouri, Iowa.

Total earnings for year ending June 30, 1910: $28,886,055.

Total Mileage: Buffalo Div., 276.6 miles; Detroit Div., 295 miles; Peru Div., 360 miles; Decatur Div., 458.9 miles; Springfield Div., 265.4 miles; Moberly Div., 858.7 miles. Total mileage 2,514.6.

Western Pacific Railway

States Served: California, Nevada, Utah.

Total earnings for year ending: N.A.

Total Mileage: San Francisco, Cal., to Salt Lake City, Utah, 921 miles; Tesla Br., 13 miles. Total mileage, 934.

Wheeling and Lake Erie Railroad

States Served: Ohio.

Total earnings for year ending June 30, 1910: $6,950,436.

Total Mileage: Toledo Div., 212 miles; Cleveland Div., 144 miles; Chagrin Falls Br., 8 miles; Ohio River Div., 13 miles; Huron Div., 13 miles; Carrollton Br., 45 miles; other branches, 47 miles. Total mileage, 482.

Here comes the *Daylight!*

Southern Pacific's new streamlined train between Los Angeles and San Francisco

Let us stand by the tracks of Southern Pacific's Coast Line, as thousands now do every day, and listen . . .

It's spring in California, and the green hills are splashed with golden poppies and blue lupine. On the white beach below, the blue surf murmurs softly.

Suddenly from far off comes a musical note, rising. Round a curve flashes a streak of color. Here comes the Daylight, *the most beautiful train in the West!*

Southern Pacific's streamlined *Daylight* is the West's newest and finest train, linking Los Angeles and San Francisco in a glorious daylight trip, streaking along the edge of the Pacific Ocean for more than a hundred breathless miles. Two identical trains give daily service in each direction. Costing $1,000,000 each, custom-built from stem to stern, they are pulled by the largest, most powerful streamlined locomotives in the world.

Step inside the *Daylight* and see the beauty and luxury that have already won the West. Notice the wide, soft seats in the coaches. They are cushioned with sponge rubber and turn to face the extraordinarily large windows. Each seat has an individual light and recessed ash tray. Note how the color scheme changes in every car, and how harmonious and restful the colors are—smoke gray, Nantes blue, French green, apricot, tan.

Here is the tavern with its big, deep semi-circular leather lounges—and the coffee shop, with a horseshoe-shaped counter where light meals are served.

Now, the diner. Observe the cheerful colors and the bright flowers on the tables. Notice that tableware and linen bear the winged *Daylight* emblem. All of it was especially designed for this train.

Finally, the parlor car, with its supremely comfortable chairs, and the parlor observation car that ends the train in a smooth, windowed curve.

THE TAVERN is a delightful place to gather with your friends. Service on the *Daylight* is characterized by real western hospitality.

The *Daylight* is, of course, completely air-conditioned. There is radio reception in every car except the diner. First class, tourist and coach tickets are all honored on the train. (Parlor cars are restricted to first class tickets, plus a nominal seat charge.)

How to see twice as much

The new *Daylight* adds a new thrill to Southern Pacific's Four Scenic Routes to California (see map). By going to California on one of these routes and returning on another one, you see *twice as much* of the West as you would by going and returning on the same route. And between Los Angeles and San Francisco you see the lovely California coast through the wide windows of the *Daylight*.

FREE TRAVEL GUIDE! Our new booklet, *How to See the Whole Pacific Coast*, describes our Four Scenic Routes and the Pacific Coast. For a free copy of this booklet and a beautiful color book describing the new *Daylight*, write O. P. Bartlett, Dept. SE-4, 310 South Michigan Avenue, Chicago.

Southern Pacific
FOUR SCENIC ROUTES
1 SHASTA ROUTE
2 OVERLAND ROUTE
3 GOLDEN STATE ROUTE
4 SUNSET ROUTE
WEST COAST OF MEXICO ROUTE
SOUTHERN PACIFIC S. LINES

EVERY SEAT on the *Daylight* is cushioned with the softest sponge rubber. There is porter service in all the coaches and parlor cars.

Southern Pacific
FOUR SCENIC ROUTES TO CALIFORNIA

APPENDIX 3
Fastest Steam Trains

Fastest Scheduled Runs in the United States
(Based on published timetables in 1950)

Railroad	Train	From/To	Dist.	Time	Speed
New York Central	Forest City	Gary/LaPorte	32.6	0.27	72.4
New York Central	Mohawk	Little Falls/Fonda	30.1	0.25	72.2

Notable Runs of Scheduled Passenger Trains for Long Distances

Date	Railroad/Train	From/To	Dist.	Time	Speed
Aug., 1894	Plant Sys. Atlantic Coast Ln	Jacksonville-Richmnd	661.5	12.51	51.48
April, 1895	Pennsylvania	Camden-Atlantic City	58.3	0.46	76.50
Sept. 1895	New York Central	New York-Buffalo	436.5	6.47	64.33
Sept. 1895	NY Central "World Flyer"	Albany-Syracuse	148.0	2.10	68.30
Feb., 1897	Burlington Route	Chicago-Denver	1,025.0	18.52	58.74
April, 1897	Lehigh Valley "Black Diamond Express"	Alpine-Geneva Junc., NY	43.9	0.33	80.00
Aug., 1897	Union Pacific	North Platte-Omaha	291.0	4.39	63.49
May, 1900	Burlington Route	Burlington-Chicago	205.8	3.08	65.50
Mar., 1902	Burlington Route	Eckley-Wray	14.8	0.90	98.70
Aug., 1902	NY Cen. "20th Century Ltd."	Kendallville-Toledo	91.0	1.15	72.80
Mar., 1903	Atlantic Coast Line	Jacksonville-Savannah	172.0	2.32	70.70
May, 1903	NY Cen. "20th Century Ltd."	Toledo-Elkhart	133.4	1.54	70.20
April, 1904	Michigan Central	Niagara Falls-Windsor	225.7	3.11	70.74
Nov., 1904	Pennsylvania	Crestline-Fort Wayne	131.0	1.53	69.56
June, 1905	Pennsylvania	Chicago-Pittsburgh	468.0	7.20	63.53
June, 1905	Lake Shore & Mich.Southern	Buffalo-Chicago	525.0	7.50	69.69
June, 1905	Pennsylvania	New York-Chicago	897.0	16.30	56.07
June, 1905	New York Central	Chicago-New York	960.5	15.56	60.28
July, 1905	Pennsylvania	Wash., O.-Ft. Wayne	81.0	1.40	75.84
Oct, 1905	Pittsburgh, Ft. Wayne & C	Crestline-Clark Junc.	257.4	3.27	74.55
Mar., 1909	New York Central	New York-Chicago	965.0	15.43	62.54

(Note: Times and speeds have, in some cases, been rounded off.)

Worst American Train Wrecks

July 17, 1856	near Philadelphia, Pa.	60
Dec. 29, 1876	Ashtabula, Ohio	84
Aug. 10, 1887	Chatsworth, Ill.	81
Oct. 10, 1888	Mud Run, Pa.,	55
Aug. 7, 1904	Eden, Col.,	96
Sept. 24, 1904	New Market, Tenn.,	56
March 16, 1906	Florence, Col.,	35
Dec. 30, 1906	Washington, D.C.	53
Jan. 2, 1907	Volland, Kans.,	33
Jan. 19, 1907	Fowler, Ind.,	29
Feb. 16, 1907	New York City	22
March 23, 1907	Colton, Calif.	26
July 20, 1907	Salem, Mich.	33
Sept. 15, 1907	Canaan, N.H.	24
March 1, 1910	Wellington, Wash.	96
March 21, 1910	Green Mountain, Iowa	55
Aug. 25, 1911	Manchester, N.Y.	27
July 4, 1912	Corning, N.Y.	40
Sept. 2, 1913	Wallingford, Conn.	21
Oct. 19, 1913	Bucatunna, Miss.	23
Aug. 5, 1914	Tipton Ford, Mo.	40
March 29, 1916	Amherst, Ohio	28
Feb. 27, 1917	Penn, Pa.	20
Dec. 20, 1917	Louisville, Ky.	41
June 22, 1918	Ivanhoe, Ind.	68
July 9, 1918	Nashville, Tenn.	101
Nov. 1, 1918	BRT Line, N.Y. (Malbourne St. Tunnel)	97
Jan. 12, 1919	South Byron, N.Y.	21
Feb. 27, 1921	Porter, Ind.	37
Aug. 6, 1922	Sulphur Springs, Mo.	40
Sept. 27, 1923	Casper, Wyo.	37
June 17, 1925	Hackettstown, N.J.	50
Dec. 23, 1926	Rockmont, Ga.,	20
June 19, 1938	Miles City, Mont.	46
Aug. 13, 1939	Carlin, Nev.	24
April 19, 1940	Little Falls, N.Y.	30
July 31, 1940	Cuyahoga Falls, Ohio	43
Nov. 9, 1941	Dunkirk, Ohio	13
Sept. 24, 1942	Dickerson, Md.	14
Dec. 27, 1942	Almonte, Ontario	34
May 23, 1943	Delair, N.J.	14
Aug. 29, 1943	Wayland, N.Y.	29
Sept. 6, 1943	Philadelphia, Pa.	79
Dec. 16, 1943	Lumberton, NC	73
July 6, 1944	High Bluff, Tenn.	35
Aug. 4, 1944	Near Stockton, Ga.	47
Sept. 14, 1944	Dewey, Inc.	29
Dec. 31, 1944	Bagley, Utah	50
June 15, 1945	Milton, Pa.	19
Aug. 9, 1945	Michigan, N. Dak.	34
April 25, 1946	Naperville, Ill.	47
Dec. 13, 1946	Guthrie, Ohio	19
Feb. 18, 1947	Gallitzin, Pa.	24
Jan. 1, 1948	Syracuse, Mo.	14
Feb. 17, 1950	Rockville Centre, N.Y.	32
Sept. 11, 1950	Nr West Lafayette, OH	33
Nov. 22, 1950	Richmond Hill, N.Y.	79
Total		2,434

Acknowledgments

The author is indebted to a number of sources for the information that appears within these covers. Particular appreciation goes to a couple of individuals who supplied material that made a real difference in the quality of the final work.

Donald W. Callender, Jr., of the Wilmington & Western Railroad, supplied several of the wonderful color photos that have been reproduced here. He is a steam enthusiast of the first water and was helpful in numerous other ways, as well. James R. Moody, one of Baltimore's crack photographers, braved record-breaking heat and humidity--to say nothing of curious crowds and showers of cinders--to get the great shots of the Strasburg Rail Road in action.

Research material for this book has come from many places other than those already mentioned. Valuable publications were used from the following sources: the Association of American Railroads, the Smithsonian Institution, the Chesapeake & Ohio Railway, the Sante Fe System, the Pennsylvania Railroad, the Norfolk and Western Railway and General Motors. In addition, the journals of the New England Railroad Club proved quite helpful, as did various editions of the World Almanac published from 1895-1911. If we have neglected to mention anyone, our apologies.

Every effort has been made to ensure that the material in this book is as accurate as possible. Any errors of fact should be brought to the attention of Bookman Publishing at the address listed in the front of the book.